ETIQUETTE GUIDE TO
KOREA

Know the rules that
make the difference!

BOYÉ LAFAYETTE DE MENTE

TUTTLE PUBLISHING
Tokyo • Rutland, Vermont • Singapore

NOTE: Unless otherwise specified, references to Korea throughout this book refer to South Korea.

Published by Tuttle Publishing, an imprint of Periplus Editions (HK) Ltd., with editorial offices at 364 Innovation Drive, North Clarendon, Vermont 05759 U.S.A.

Library of Congress Cataloging-in-Publication Data
De Mente, Boye.
  Etiquette guide to Korea : know the rules that make the difference / Boye Lafayette De Mente.
    p. cm.
  Includes index.
  ISBN 978-0-8048-3948-8 (pbk. : alk. paper)
  1. Etiquette–Korea. 2. Korea–Social life and customs. I. Title.
  BJ2007.C56D42 2008
  395.095–dc22   2007037118

ISBN 978-0-8048-3948-8

Distributed by:
**North America, Latin America
& Europe**
Tuttle Publishing
364 Innovation Drive
North Clarendon, VT 05759-9436 U.S.A.
Tel: 1 (802) 773-8930
Fax: 1 (802) 773-6993
info@tuttlepublishing.com
www.tuttlepublishing.com

Asia Pacific
Berkeley Books Pte. Ltd.
61 Tai Seng Avenue #02-12
Singapore 534167
Tel: (65) 6280-1330
Fax (65) 6280-6290
inquiries@periplus.com.sg
www.periplus.com

Japan
Tuttle Publishing
Yaekari Building, 3rd Floor
5-4-12 Osaki, Shinagawa-ku
Tokyo 141 0032 Japan
Tel: (81) 3 5437-0171
Fax: (81) 3 5437-0755
tuttle-sales@gol.com

First edition
11 10 09 08   6 5 4 3 2 1

Printed in Singapore

TUTTLE PUBLISHING® is a registered trademark of Tuttle Publishing, a division of Periplus Editions (HK) Ltd.

Contents

Preface

Introduction

Part I

Part II

Part III

Part IV

Useful Expressions and Selected Vocabulary
Common Expressions

Preface

The "Hermit Kingdom" in Its Modern Splendor!

South Korea is a tiny nation on the southern half of the Korean Peninsula that has one of the largest economies in the world and is home to huge industrial conglomerates that sell high-tech products worldwide.

The astounding development of this economic powerhouse— which began only in 1952—has made South Korea a world-class destination for businesspeople, tourists, sports enthusiasts, and students.

Known as "the Hermit Kingdom" until the final decades of the nineteenth century because it kept its doors closed to the outside world, Korea wasn't exposed to international influences until the middle of the twentieth century. Perhaps this is why much of Korea's traditional culture has been preserved in spite of the explosion of modernity the nation has undergone. Today Korea's age-old culture has combined with ultramodern Western ways and conveniences to transform the country into one of the world's most popular destinations.

Tourism is now one of Korea's largest industries, thanks to the country's unique history and living culture, extraordinary shopping opportunities, and amazing scenic beauty. The Seoul

Olympics, held in 1988, attracted more than two million foreign visitors. Today the number of tourists entering Korea each year is well over six million and growing. In addition, several hundred thousand businesspeople also visit Korea annually.

The traditional Korean custom of extending effusive hospitality and goodwill to guests makes Korea a kind of visitors' paradise. This is only enhanced by the inherent honesty of Korea's people and the nation's high sanitation standards, around-the-clock public security, excellent accommodations, outstanding transportation systems, and service that is among the best in the world.

But these are not the most important of Korea's attractions. What visitors find the most enticing about Korea are cultural things unique to the country—arts and crafts, cuisine, traditional apparel, historical artifacts, festivals, and traditional sports and entertainment. There is an aura and a mystique that exudes from all of these things, giving Korea a special allure that is indefinable but touches everyone.

And finally, there are the people themselves—charming, vibrant, and dignified. The friendships visitors make in Korea and the cross-cultural experiences they have there are often the highlights of their trips.

To get the most out of a visit to Korea, whether made for business or pleasure, it is important to know a great deal about the history, values, attitudes, and behavior of its people. In this book I have attempted to identify and explain the cultural elements that make up the personal and business etiquette of Koreans, with insights and advice on how to interact with them appropriately and successfully.

Boyé Lafayette De Mente

Travel Notes

Korea can be reached by air from every major capital in the world, either through direct or connecting flights from international airports in East Asia. Some 40 international airlines provide regular services to and from Korea, with over 1,500 flights per week.

There are eight international airports in Korea: Incheon and Gimpo airports, serving Seoul; Gimhae, serving Busan (Pusan); Jeju, serving Jeju (Cheju) Island; and Cheongju, Daegu, Yangyang, and Gwangju airports, serving the cities after which they are named. Most international visitors to Korea arrive at Incheon Airport.

A limousine bus company provides service to and from Incheon Airport and all major hotels in Seoul. There are also special airport and city buses that leave from various points in Seoul for Incheon, and a rail and subway line that connects Incheon with Gimpo Airport and Seoul.

A Korea City Air Terminal (KCAT) in Seoul's Gangnam business district provides limousine bus service to and from Incheon Airport, and provides check-in service and passport clearance for departing passengers. The commute between Incheon Airport and KCAT is about 60 minutes.

Various ship lines also provide passenger service to Korea. Among those from the American West Coast are Waterman Steamship, American Pioneer, Pacific Far East, Pacific Orient Express, State Marine, and United States Lines. Several ferry companies including Bu Gwan Ferry, Korea Ferry, and Korea Marine Express provide regular services linking Busan and Jeju Island with the Japanese ports of Shimonoseki, Kobe, and Hakata. Another ferry line travels between Incheon and the Chinese ports of Tianjin and Weihai.

The Korean Language

Unlike citizens of other Asian countries, all Koreans speak and write the same language, which has been a crucial factor in their strong national identity. Although there are several Korean dialects in addition to the standard one used in Seoul and other central areas, they are similar enough that people do not have trouble understanding each other.

In spite of this linguistic unity, aspects of the Korean language can be confusing to both Koreans and foreigners. Depending on the region and the speaker, there can be subtle differences in the pronunciation of several sounds basic to the language—resulting in different spellings when the words in question are transcribed in the Roman letters familiar to Westerners. Another factor that causes confusion is the use of more than one system of spelling the language in Roman letters. In the past many such systems were used. Today two remain: One created in the early twentieth century by George M. McCune and Edwin O. Reischauer—Americans who grew up in Asia as the children of missionaries—and one devised more recently by a government-sponsored committee of scholars.

The government system is the official one, but the McCune-Reischauer system is far easier for Americans and Europeans to recognize and use, and it is favored by many, including Koreans who are involved with the outside world. In many cases, I have chosen to use the McCune-Reischauer system of spelling Korean terms because otherwise they would not be recognized by many foreigners.

The Korean language is written in three different ways: with Chinese ideograms called *hantcha* (hahn-chah), or Chinese characters; with a purely Korean alphabet created by scholars in the fifteenth century called *hangul* (hahn-guhl), or Korean writing; and with Roman letters, as discussed above. Most public signs are written in *hangul* script.

The Chinese *hantcha* system of writing prevailed well into modern times, especially among members of the upper class. In the 1980s the government attempted to eliminate the use of *hantcha*, but these efforts were generally ignored by the public and the attempt was dropped. Now approximately 1,800 *hantcha* are taught in Korean schools. Most Korean names are still written with Chinese characters.

Pronouncing Korean Words

There is a clear distinction between vowels and consonants in the Korean language, and there is no exact equivalent for some of them in English speech. The following pronunciation guides are close enough that you will generally be understood when you use them.

VOWELS	
a	**ah**
ya	**yah**
eo	**awe**
yeo	**yah**
o	**oh**
yo	**yoh**
u	**uuh**
yu	**you**
eu	**uu**
i	**ee**
ae	**an**
yae	**yay**
e	**eh**
ye	**yeh**
oe	**weh**
wi	**we**
eui	**ea**
wa	**wah**
wae	**wea**
weo	**waw**
we	**weh**

CONSONANTS	
k	**k** *or* **g**
g	**g**
n	**n**
t	**t** *or* **d**
d	**d**
r	*close to* **t** *sound or soft* **d**
m	**m**
p	**pp** *or* **bb**
s	**s**
ng	**ing**
ch	**ch** *or* **j**
j	**j**
ch'	**ch**
k'	**k**
t'	**t**
p'	**p** *as in puff*
h	**h**
kk	**ch**
tt	**tt**
pp	**pp**
ss	**see**
jj	**g**

Introduction

From an Age of Repression to an Age of Miracles

It is impossible to understand and appreciate Korea without knowing something about the history of the peninsula and its people. It is, in fact, one of the most remarkable sagas in the annals of humanity.

Archeological findings indicate that ancestors of modern-day Koreans began arriving on the peninsula somewhere between 40,000 and 20,000 years ago.* (There is some evidence that very early human beings lived on the peninsula 600,000 years ago!) The earliest Koreans are believed to have been migrants and invaders from present-day Manchuria, northern China, and Mongolia. Historians say these early arrivals consisted of extended kin groups or clans who practiced shamanism, a belief system that centers on the worship of nature and ancestral spirits. These ancient clan groups were to survive and persist as a major factor in Korean life into modern times.

---

* Ancient human footprints fossilized in stone have been found on Korea's famous resort island of Cheju. Sharp and perfectly clear, the footprints measure 8½ inches by 10 inches! Another extraordinary sign of the antiquity and racial uniqueness of the Korean people is the fact that about half of them do not have apocrine glands—the glands that produce body odor.

According to legend, the state of Korea was founded in 2333 BC by a mythical figure named Dangun.

In 109 BC the famous Chinese emperor Wu-Ti, also known as the Martial Emperor, ushered in 400 years of Chinese hegemony when he invaded and captured Wiman Chosun, the largest of the existing clan kingdoms on the Koran peninsula. After this conquest, large numbers of Chinese administrators, artists, craftsmen, scholars, and religious leaders took up residence in Nangnang, near present-day Pyongyang, turning it into a thriving center of Chinese culture. The Korean clan kingdoms adopted the Chinese forms of Confucian-based government, etiquette, and ethics. Learning and knowledge were emphasized, as was the value of precise personal and public relationships.

As the decades under Chinese hegemony passed Korea's multiple small clan fiefdoms were consolidated into three nation states: Shilla, Koguryo, and Paekche. Shilla was founded in 57 BC in the southeast; Koguryo, located in the northern part of the peninsula and in what is now Manchuria, was founded in 37 BC; and Paekche, in the southwest, was founded in 18 BC. From the fourth century to the middle of the seventh century AD these three kingdoms competed for control of the peninsula. In AD 660 Paekche was annexed by Shilla. In 668, Koguryo, in collaboration with members of Shilla, emerged as a unified political entity under the flag of the Shilla Kingdom.

In the mid eighth century, however, central authority again began to decline. The unified Koguryo-Shilla Kingdom was overturned in 935 by a new dynasty that took the name Koryo, from which the word *Korea* is derived.

Buddhism, first introduced in Korea several hundred years earlier by Chinese monks, was made the state religion of Koryo. Nevertheless, shamanism continued to be the primary religion of the clans and is still evident today in the form of rituals and festivals that overshadow Buddhism.

In the thirteenth century the Mongolian warlord Kublai Khan, who had already conquered China and established the Yuan Dynasty, invaded Koryo and turned it into a vassal state. As generations passed both the political and religious institutions of Koryo became increasingly corrupt and inefficient. The Yuan Dynasty of Mongols in China also became week and ineffective.

In 1390 a group of rebel Koryo officials led by a general named Yi (Lee) Sung-Gye allied with the leaders of China's newly established Ming Dynasty to overthrow the Mongol-dominated Koryo government.

In 1392 a new dynasty was established in Korea, returning Chinese influence to the peninsula. To claim antiquity for the regime, the new Yi Dynasty adopted the name *Chosun*, recalling one of Korea's most ancient clans. Seoul became Korea's capital—as it would remain to the present day.

General Yi, who had himself crowned King Taejo, decreed that an extreme version of Confucianism would thereafter be the foundation for Korean society as a whole—from the form and function of the government down to the structure of individual families in which fathers and senior males were supreme and virtually all individual thought and behavior by other family members was banned.

This newly established political and social ideology quickly replaced Buddhism as the state religion. It called for precise etiquette that mandated the use of respect language, the already universal bow, and personal behavior specifically tailored to social rank. In addition, it decreed ancestor worship to be a foundation of Korean society, required that the sexes be segregated in their living quarters, and established a precise system of gender- and hierarchy-based etiquette that became firmly embedded in Korea's culture during the early centuries of the dynasty. These things remain important to this day.

The first decades of the new dynasty were a golden age of artistic and scientific achievement that saw amazing advances in astronomy, diet, medicine, meteorology, and printing (including woodblock type). During this era and other long periods in Korean history, creativity, invention, and innovation flourished, putting Korea's legacy on a par with the early accomplishments of the Middle East and Europe.

Oddly enough, however, the very same Confucian ideology that had driven Koreans to excel for nearly a thousand years was to act as a double-edged sword during the final centuries of the Chosun Dynasty. Instead of continuing to encourage and reward innovation, the government began putting overwhelming emphasis on maintaining the status quo and revering the past, stifling creativity and resulting in the country gradually becoming frozen in time.

Factionalism rising out of the deeply embedded clan mentality of leaders on every social and governmental level was also a major factor in the decline of the creative spirit and ambitions of Koreans. This factionalism divided the leadership of the Chosun Dynasty, demoralized its military forces, and left the country defenseless against outside invasion—first by Japan in the late sixteenth century and then again in the late nineteenth century, when Japan, Russia, and European powers all vied for control of the peninsula.

In 1910 Japan annexed Korea and turned it into a colony, formally ending the Chosun Dynasty. Under Japanese rule all civil liberties were revoked. The Japanese closed most private schools and established their own Japanese-language public school system to assimilate Korean youth into Japanese culture. Korean employees and others who came into daily contact with Japanese were required to speak the Japanese language and behave in a Japanese manner. The goal of the Japanese was to totally eliminate Korean culture.

Koreans fought this assimilation process in every way they could. Resistance movements were formed among students, factory workers, and urban intellectuals. In 1919 the Japanese police and army crushed nationwide demonstrations in which about 370,000 Koreans participated, and some 6,670 were killed.

In spite of the valiant efforts of many Koreans, outside intervention would be required to free Korea from Japanese rule. At a 1943 meeting in Cairo the leaders of the United States, Great Britain, and China declared that Korea's independence should be restored as soon as World War II ended.

The two Koreas we know today were created after Japan's surrender and the end of the war. On August 24, 1945, United States president Harry Truman authorized a line of demarcation that allowed Soviet forces to accept the surrender of Japanese troops north of the 38th parallel, with United States forces accepting those to the south. However, the Soviets and their Korean communist allies led by Kim Il-Sung quickly turned the 38th parallel into a heavily armed barrier between the northern and southern halves of the country.

In November 1947 the United Nations (UN) adopted a resolution stipulating that representatives of the Korean people should establish conditions for unifying the two parts of their country and establishing a new government. The Soviets refused to admit a UN commission to observe elections in the north, so in May 1948 elections were held only in the peninsula's southern half. A formerly self-exiled political activist named Syngman Rhee was elected president of the new country, and in July 1948 Southern leaders adopted a new democratic constitution. On August 15 the Republic of Korea was established without any participation by North Korea.

Although the Japanese had left Korea, peace proved to be elusive. During the next year the United States withdrew all of its troops from the southern half of the peninsula, except for a 500-person military advisory group. Kim Il-Sung, still the leader of the communist north, seized what appeared to be an opportunity to unite the peninsula under his rule. On June 25, 1950, he sent his huge army across the 38th parallel in a surprise invasion of the new Republic of Korea, beginning what would be known as the Korean War.

On June 27, 1950, the UN Security Council requested that members of the UN assist South Korea. The United States, initially responding with air and naval support, committed ground forces by the end of the month, but not before the North Koreans had captured all of South Korea except for its southern tip.

Fifteen other nations soon joined the United States under the flag of the UN. The North Korean forces were pushed back across the 38th parallel and up to the Yalu River—the border between North Korea and China. This resulted in China joining North Korea to fight against the United States and its allies, bringing the war to a stalemate.

On July 27, 1953, an armistice signed by North Korea and South Korea and its allies stopped the fighting. But it did not and still has not resulted in the reunification of South Korea and North Korea.

Korea in the Modern World

South Korea's development into an economic superpower began shortly after the end of the Korean War, and is one of the miracles of the twentieth century. It was made possible because, with the introduction of democracy and freedom from outside invasion, ordinary Koreans were able for the first time in some 400 years to make full use of their Confucian-oriented etiquette and ethics. In combination with the incredible energy, creativity, diligence, dedication, and ambition that had been suppressed since the early decades of the backward-looking Chosun Dynasty, this proved to be a powerful driving force.

Beginning in 1952, the rapid industrialization and urbanization of South Korea fundamentally changed all three basic elements of life—housing, clothing, and food. Instead of living with generations of relatives, many Koreans now share homes with only their nuclear families. Western dress has become commonplace. And while rice remains a staple food for many older Koreans, the younger generations generally prefer Western-style food. Among the most dramatic social and cultural changes resulting from this new economic environment were a birth-control drive that reduced the average family size from seven or eight children to less than two, and new family-related laws that ensured equality for sons and daughters in matters of inheritance.

During this time, Korea's economy became internationally oriented to an extraordinary degree. This was brought about in part by the foresight of the founders of Korean conglomerates such as Samsung, LG, Daewoo, and Hyundai, who in the late 1950s were the first Asians to send their sons to business schools and universities in the United States and Europe to prepare them for careers in international business. Ever since, large numbers of Koreans have spent time abroad either as students or expatriate employees of Korea's large multinational corporations. This has resulted in a growing community of people who have had years or even decades of experience interacting with foreign businesspeople from around the world. These Koreans speak fair to very good English and behave very much like Americans and other Westerners in personal situations.

Nevertheless, even these "internationalized" people conform to characteristic Korean customs and etiquette when interacting with other Koreans who have not been directly exposed to Western attitudes, particularly in the workplace. In spite of a recent history full of foreign invasions and occupation,

Koreans have always had a distinctive character impervious to outside influence. Powerful elements of this unique Korean culture continue to influence the thinking and behavior of the Korean people.

Today's Korea is still one of the most homogeneous countries in the world, racially and linguistically. It has its own culture, language, traditional dress, and cuisine, all of which are separate and distinct from those of its neighboring countries.

Hard work, filial piety, and modesty remain characteristics esteemed by Koreans. They are proud of their traditional culture, their astounding economic success, and their upscale lifestyle.

The Korean Wave

In response to a propensity among the country's leading manufacturers and others to downplay or conceal their Korean identity, by the end of the 1990s many Koreans began to emphasize the importance of maintaining elements of the traditional customs that had added so much to their lives. The Korean Ministry of Culture and Tourism picked up on this movement and inaugurated a series of ongoing programs under the banner of *Hallyu* (Hahl-l'yuu), or "the Korean Wave."

This was intended not only to preserve the most desirable elements of Korean culture, but also to emphasize the domestic and international advantages of displaying Korea's traditional culture rather than hiding it.

Six unique elements make up the Korean Wave. They are referred to as "Korean brands": *hangul* (hahn-guhl), the purely Korean alphabet and writing system; *hansik* (hahn-sheek), traditional Korean food; *hanbok* (hahn-boak), traditional Korean attire; *hanok* (hahn-oak), traditional Korean housing; *hanji* (hahn-jee), the distinctive Korean paper made of mulberry; and *hankuk eumak* (hahn-kuuk uu-mahk), traditional Korean music.

Marketing for Korean products around the world and the promotion of Korea as a tourist destination now incorporate several or all of these six unique elements of the Korean Wave.

The results of this program have been astounding. By the turn of the twenty-first century popular Korean music and historical dramas had millions of dedicated fans in neighboring Japan. Japanese entrepreneurs by the thousands jumped on the Korean Wave, opening traditionally styled Korean shops and restaurants in Tokyo, Osaka, and many other Japanese cities. In addition, an influx of Japanese tourists poured into Korea, becoming one of the most remarkable developments in the relationship between the two countries since the seventh century AD, when Koreans acted as conduits in bringing Chinese culture to Japan. Now cultural exchange between these former enemies is growing exponentially, amazing history buffs familiar with their historical relationship.

Less remarkable but equally fascinating has been the spread of the Korean Wave into China, Thailand, Vietnam, and other Southeast Asian countries. In Vietnam the hanbok has become a national hit as a wedding gown. In Thailand products emblazoned with *hangul* are selling like the proverbial hotcakes.

The Korean Wave (with "Korean Sense" as a subtitle) has become the symbol of the new Korea, merging its culture and commerce into a powerful force the likes of which has not been seen in the country since the heyday of the great Shilla Dynasty.

Part I

The Character and Personality of Koreans

In the past hundred years, Korea has undergone immense changes: from an isolated nation to an international power-house, and from an agricultural society to a business-minded culture of giant mega-corporations. In this country that respects the value of tradition and history, however, some unique cultural elements have remained to influence the way Koreans approach life. The following sections discuss some of the most important of these elements.

Although some are not as important today as they once were, these beliefs and practices remain distinctive features of Korean behavior, and foreigners must know about them to understand and deal appropriately and effectively with Koreans.

Love for the Korean Nation

The last line of the Korean national anthem, "Aegukga" (Aye-gook-gah), or "Love the Country," does more to explain the pride and passion that Koreans take in their nation than anything else I can think of. It goes like this: "Let us love—come grief, come gladness—this, our beloved land!"

To fully appreciate this love of country, you have to be Korean—to know Korea's history, its glories, and its tragedies. Over the past two-and-a-half millennia Korea has been invaded and occupied by the Chinese, the Mongols, and the Japanese, and when not fighting outsiders the nation was savaged by internal regional conflicts. But despite these travails, Korea produced some of the world's greatest works of art, created masterpieces of poetry, and made many technical advances far earlier than any other people.

Another reason for the pride Koreans take in their homeland is the extraordinary scenic beauty of the Korean peninsula. This feeling is especially powerful because the native shamanistic religion of the Koreans, like those of the early Japanese and American Indians, included the belief that people were a part of nature, and that recognizing and respecting its beauty was a key part of their being.

Knowing how Koreans feel about *Hanguk* (hahn-guuk), the Korean nation, and fully respecting this feeling can be a major asset for foreigners visiting and living in Korea.

The Remarkable *Han* Element

A key cultural factor that played a fundamental role in South Korea's incredible rise is subsumed in the word *han* (hahn), which Korean scholars translate as "unrequited resentments." This requires explanation, because it means much more than what this English phrase suggests.

Han can be understood to encompass all of the ambitions, emotions, desires, spirit, and intellectual impulses that were prohibited and oppressed from the beginning of the Chosun Dynasty in 1392 until the 1950s. When South Koreans were freed from political oppression, all of these repressed things were released and provided the energy, power, and passion they devoted to creating a modern economy. The power of *han* has not yet expended itself, and the ferocity, dedication, and diligence with which the people work must be seen to be believed.

(North Koreans, on the other hand, remain beaten down and mired in the mud of the past by their misguided Communist overlords. They have not yet been freed from the chains of *han*.)

Korea's National Slogan

As the world is now very much aware, Koreans have a work ethic and competitive spirit that is virtually unbounded. This is embodied in one of the most commonly heard expressions in the country—*Yolshimhi hapsida*! (Yohl-sheem-hee hahp-she-dah!), or "Let's do our best!" In fact, this might even be called the country's national slogan. And as Koreans have demonstrated in so many ways, their best is very good—as is now further evidenced by the spreading Korean Wave.

Harmony and Korean Etiquette

The earliest extensive reports on Korean etiquette and ethics were written by members of the Chinese military, and later by the administrators posted in Korea during the centuries following the 109 BC conquest of the peninsula by Chinese forces. These reports enthusiastically described Korea as a country of *hwa* (whah), or harmony. But the harmony that existed in Korea wasn't harmony in the Western sense: In its Chinese and Korean context, *hwa* means never saying or doing anything that contradicts the etiquette and ethics prescribed by Confucianism. The visitors from China were enormously impressed by the way Koreans fulfilled the mandates of Confucianism regarding proper etiquette, speech, and behavior as determined by personal relationships, age, gender, social class, business or official rank, and so on.

Although at that point Confucianism had been only recently introduced in Korea, it was already a key part of the country's culture. The Koreans' ready adoption of this Confucian-oriented harmony had no doubt been expedited by their shamanistic beliefs and practices, which were based on living in harmony with nature and one another. In fact, Koreans were so diligent in their adoption of Confucianism that they eventually became even more Confucian-oriented than the Chinese, who were Confucianism's first proponents.

However, Korea's all-important Confucian-based harmony was traditionally built on an authoritarian, hierarchical etiquette that had very little to do with the actual feelings and desires of the individuals involved. Structure and form took precedent over people's natural instincts and inclinations.

Although still vital to an understanding of Korean culture, the drive to maintain harmony is not nearly as important today as it was in earlier times.

Korea's Shame Culture

Sociologists describe Korea as having a "shame culture," in contrast to the religion-oriented "guilt cultures" that predominate in the West.

Shame cultures are based on conformity to prescribed etiquette, behavior that is visible and can be instantly measured. Instead of being programmed by religion to feel guilty as a result of wrongdoing and to fear punishment by secular and religious authorities—both in this life and in whatever may come after it—Koreans were conditioned to feel intense shame in this life. This turned out to be a more powerful control mechanism than internal guilt, and resulted in individual Koreans being far better behaved than their religiously oriented counterparts.

Korea's shame culture was derived from the influence of Confucianism, which taught that the rules of etiquette and personal shame should be the basis of all morality—not religious or secular laws. Shame, or *changpi* (chahng-pee), was everywhere; it was imposed on violators of the strict rules of etiquette by all of their society and culture. In contrast, guilt cultures depended primarily on the dissemination and enforcement of legal or religious organizations.

In earlier times a terrible punishment could be meted out to Koreans who shamed themselves by failing to live up to the standards of etiquette: they could be cast out by their families. Without family they had no identity and no security, and these outcasts became more like living ghosts than people.

Still today the fear of shame is a major factor in the high standards of etiquette and group responsibility that are integral parts of the Korean character. But now, in part at least, shame is just as likely to be the result of failing to live up to one's personal ambitions as it is to be the result of failing to maintain standards of etiquette. It is the fear of shaming themselves and their families combined with culturally driven ambition that compels Koreans to strive as mightily as they can to get the best possible education, the best possible job, and to do their best in everything they set out to do.

The shame orientation of Korean culture is weaker today than it used to be, but by Western standards it is still incredibly strong. When Koreans misbehave in any way or fail in any enterprise their feelings of shame are powerful. When they are shamed by someone else's behavior toward them, their sense of shame is generally even stronger and invariably calls for some kind of response.

It is important for foreigners dealing with Koreans to know enough about their culture to be aware of the kinds of things that result in shame, including not using proper respect language toward a senior or an elder, not following the prescribed form of greeting, failing to receive high marks in school, not achieving personal goals, and so on.

Rank Has Its Privileges

R ank is a primary foundation of strict hierarchical societies and of vital importance in them. You must know or quickly learn the rank of everyone around you because their rank must determine your language and behavior toward them, and it impacts how they will treat you.

Until well into the twentieth century Korea had one of the most hierarchical societies in the world. People belonged to specific classes and categories within classes that were structured on an inferior-superior basis with very precise and very strict rules controlling behavior.

Although considerably diminished today, rank consciousness is still an important facet of Korean culture.

Dignity in Korean Culture

W *iom* (we-ohm), or dignity, is a vital element in the character of Koreans. Its importance developed because traditionally the only thing common Koreans had control of and could make choices about was their dignity. This served as the foundation of their face, or their personal value as it was represented to the world through their status and adherence to etiquette.

Koreans maintained their dignity by scrupulously obeying all of the demands of their strict code of etiquette and doing whatever they could to prevent others from damaging their self-image, their face, their reputation. Thus, individuals took any perceived slight to their dignity seriously, and acted to protect it at all costs.

The extraordinary sensitivity of individual Koreans to this culturally programmed need for dignity has been diminishing since the mid twentieth century, but it remains a significant part of their national character.

The Importance of Saving Face

The importance of social class and rank in premodern Korea meant that one had to know and follow precise forms of behavior to avoid offending others. Doing something that made you or someone else lose face was not a trivial thing. It could be, and often was, disastrous. This made Koreans incredibly sensitive about their own behavior and the behavior of others, because there were so many things that could get them into trouble.

This gave birth to *chae-myun* (chay-m'yuun), or "face-saving," one of the most important and demanding aspects of life in Korea. In short, face-saving was based on not doing or saying anything that might embarrass other people or make them feel bad.

Today *chae-myum* continues to be a major factor in all relationships in Korea, particularly in a work environment.

Korea's Power Culture

Broadly speaking, Koreans are obsessed with *kwollyok* (kwohl-yoak), or authority and power. Korean culture has always been a "power culture," from the top of the government down to individual households where senior males had the first and last word. Until the end of World War II and the establishment of a democratic government in South Korea, only a tiny percentage of people—all men—had any sort of authority or power at all.

Before 1945, it often didn't make any difference how educated or skilled people were or how hard they worked. Only power over others made it possible for Koreans to guarantee their security or improve their standard of living. In South Korea's modern society, however, power can be achieved through study, work, and accumulation of wealth.

The desire for power is one of the primary motivating factors in how hard Koreans study and work. And once a Korean has power, he or she is understandably reluctant to give it up.

Education in Korea

In modern-day Korea, education is highly valued as the path to power, money, status, and success—and there are few people as driven to succeed as South Koreans.

However, education in Korea has been obsolete for decades: The traditional learn-by-rote educational system created and controlled by the government since ancient times ignores and stifles innovation and entrepreneurship by emphasizing memorization over understanding and thinking for oneself.

This has led a growing number of parents to send their children to alternative schools in addition to the official public ones. After regular school lets out at 3 PM, hundreds of thousands of students eat a quick dinner before rushing to one of thousands of private cram schools spread throughout the country. There they spend an additional five hours a day studying a variety of subjects, including English.

Many of these students eventually go on to high schools and universities abroad. There are now some quarter million Korean students receiving education overseas, "voting with their feet against the present educational system," according to a Hongik University professor. Koreans are the third largest contingent of foreign students in the United States, surpassed in number only by students from China and India—nations with populations 20 times larger than that of Korea.

Not surprisingly, there is now a growing movement among businesspeople, educators, and parents to bring the Korean educational system up to date and take it out of the hands of government bureaucrats. In the meanwhile, though, this exodus to overseas educational opportunities is ensuring that Korea's younger generations are internationally minded and familiar with varied cultures, including that of the West.

The Vital Role of Sincerity

When Koreans meet new people their cultural antenna is always up. This antenna reads many things, one of the most important of which is subsumed in the word *chinshim* (cheen-sheem), "true heart" or sincerity.

To Koreans, *chinshim* refers to a wide range of things—character in general, as well as philosophical, spiritual, and ethical considerations—that must be of a high order to be acceptable, much less impressive. *Chinshim* is important in Korea for historical reasons: For millennia there were no laws that guaranteed personal rights or protected the people. In that environment things most Westerners took for granted in their relationships were uncommon—including courteous and helpful treatment by officials, being able to confidently do business with people they did not know, and the ability to develop personal relationships without spending large amounts of time and money. Success—in life and in business—therefore depended heavily on the sincerity of the people with whom one interacted.

Like many traditionally Korean cultural attributes, concern with *chinshim* has decreased since the mid 1900s. Nevertheless, it remains an important part of life in Korea. Companies interviewing potential employees, for example, evaluate a number of things—the applicant's name (which tells an enormous amount about the history of his or her family), what region of the country he or she was born in (also historically meaningful), and the level of his or her *chinshim*.

Cultivating Friendships

Friendships are obviously important for both business and social reasons in virtually all societies, but in few cultures do people go as far as Koreans to develop and keep friendships, or *ujong* (uu-johng).

This extraordinary behavior is rooted in the Koreans' historical inability to depend on anyone except those with whom they had close personal or family ties. In personal, professional, and governmental spheres friendship and emotion were primary motivators, not responsibility. Strangers could not be counted on for anything, even services that local officials and bureaucrats were obliged by custom and law to provide. This made it necessary to have close friendships with a wide variety of people who could provide the necessary protection and services to allow one to live a safe, healthy, and successful life.

The legacy of this social conditioning is still very much alive when it comes to friends and friendships in Korea. Koreans, especially businesspeople, go out of their way to develop and maintain a circle of friends because it is invariably through friends that they are able to get things done. Foreigners in Korea generally discover that they must do the same in order to be successful there.

The "Someone You Know" Factor

The imperative of having many close friendships is influenced by *anun saram* (ah-nuun sah-rahm), which can be interpreted as "someone you know."

Historically, the collective and exclusive nature of Korean families often made it dangerous or virtually impossible for individuals to interact with people they did not know and were not related to. This arose in part from an inability to make private or public commitments to outsiders, because any commitment would impact one's whole family—and sometimes one's whole clan. This resulted in individual Koreans being wary of people with whom they had no family relationship, even to the point of avoiding contact with such individuals.

But when contact with outsiders was required, the only way to get things done was to develop close relationships with them. It would then be safe to deal with these people in both business and personal arenas.

Anun saram is no longer vitally important to the thinking and behavior of Koreans, but foreigners wanting to do business in Korea should still be intimately familiar with this cultural factor and go out of their way to develop close personal relationships with those they want to do business with.

Clans in Korean Society

Another important element in Korean society is the clan factor. Koreans trace their history back to just a few dozen family clans that entered the peninsula from the north and northwest thousands of years ago. Over the millennia these *chok* (chak) or clans grew, and although they eventually spread throughout the peninsula they remained intact and fiercely protective of their identities, their names, and the regions first settled by their ancestors. The largest and most powerful clans formed the peninsula's first kingdoms—Koguryo, Paekche, and Shilla.

Although this ancient clan system has survived into modern times and its powerful families still make up most of the country's elite, its influence is now overshadowed by democracy, individualism, and a highly industrialized economy. But the clan structure is still important in matters of marriage, employment, and political success. These clan relationships also impact the way Koreans behave toward other Koreans. Their interaction is determined by the statuses of their families and clan names, as well as their birthplaces and the schools they attended.

Foreigners who deal with Koreans, particularly in a business environment, would be wise to make themselves aware of the clan relationships of their contacts and diplomatically sound them out about their family histories. These things will influence their willingness and ability to interact with other Koreans.

The Korean Family

There is a lot of talk in the United States and other Western countries about the importance of the family, but the Western concept of family and its role in society pales in comparison to the Korean one.

To appreciate the importance and power of family in Korea one must fully understand the Korean term *chib* (cheeb), which literally means "household." In essence this word does not clearly distinguish between the individuals in the family and the family as a unit. This is indicative of the traditional sense of responsibility in Korean families, which was collective: each member was responsible for the family and the family was responsible for each member.

From childhood Koreans were required to think and behave in ways that would protect their *chib*, avoid dishonoring it, and ensure its continuity. One could say that this intense group orientation meant that, in the Western sense, individuals did not exist in traditional Korean society.

Another influential aspect of the traditional Korean family structure is its hierarchical nature, which was a building block of Korea's social and political orders. Like family life, these larger systems were based on absolute submission of inferiors to superiors.

The role and importance of the family is still a major factor in Korean society, and although its power has weakened significantly since the mid twentieth century, family is still far more important in Korea than it is in most other countries. Adult Koreans will still almost always consult with their families to get approval before making decisions about work and personal matters, among other things.

Women in Korea

In the past Korean women lived restricted and secluded lives. Most urban women never spoke to or spent time with anyone who wasn't a member of their own family. For one long period in Korea's recent history, women in urban areas could not even leave their family compounds during the day to shop or pay social visits. They were allowed to leave only for a few hours at night, hours when men were required to stay indoors in order to keep the two sexes segregated. And it was virtually forbidden for anyone to use a woman's given name, which resulted in many women living out their entire lives without hearing their names spoken aloud. Instead, they were referred to according to their relationship with the speaker and the members of their families.

These strict political and social controls were abolished near the end of the nineteenth century, but it was to be several decades before women in Korea felt able to exercise the kind of personal freedoms Americans and others took for granted.

Today, Korean women are among the freest and most aggressive women in the world, and they have played an important role in their country's astounding economic success. Their presence and influence is seen in virtually every industry and profession.

Statistically, women compose 38 percent of the college and university students in Korea and 16 percent of university faculty. They account for half of all college and university graduates, hold 35 percent of the information technology jobs in the country, and make up 45 percent of its Internet users. In Korea 47 percent of all women who are of age are employed. Female-owned and female-managed businesses, including some large-scale firms, are common. Women are especially prominent in foreign companies in Korea, as well as in the service industries that cater to travelers.

On individual and personal levels Korean women often enjoy freedoms and opportunities equal to those of Korean men. But although they have basically the same legal rights as men, their culture's Confucian traditions continue to make Korea a man's country by permitting the same kind of discrimination and abuse against women that is common in the United States and other Western nations. In response there are several national women's organizations that work to ensure the rights of women in all areas of Korean society. There are even advocacy groups organized against the lack of protection for women working in Korea's organized sex industry.

One of the more prominent women's organizations in Korea is the Korean Women's Development Institute, which conducts research and studies on women, provides education and training for women, and assists in women's activities.

The Self-sufficiency Syndrome

Throughout much of their nation's long history there was no government backup and no social security system that Koreans could depend on to rescue them in times of need. Individual families, and by extension the clans to which they belonged, were on their own: instead of relying on a central government each family, each village, and each region relied on itself. *Chakupjachok* (chah-kuup-jah-choke) or "self-sufficiency" became deeply ingrained in the Korean mindset.

Another primary factor in the growth of this essential part of the Korean character was Korea's geographic and economic isolation throughout its early history—notwithstanding contacts with China and Japan, which were essentially only cultural.

In the post–Korean War business world *chakupjachok* resulted in larger companies becoming conglomerates that were as close as possible to totally self-sufficient. This included the sourcing of raw materials for and the manufacturing of their own goods, as well as doing their own advertising, marketing, wholesaling, retailing, and product after-service. The effectiveness of this approach is evidenced today by tiny Korea's status as one of the world's leading economic superpowers.

(The self-sufficiency syndrome has also influenced life in North Korea, where it was taken to an extreme. It was a key factor in the policies of North Korea's leaders and contributed to economic disaster on a massive scale. The communist government refused to allow foreign investments in the country and did not allow its people to engage in entrepreneurial types of business. It was not until near the end of the twentieth century that North Korea's rulers began gradually allowing the adoption of features of a market economy.)

The drive toward self-sufficiency continues to influence Korea's policies dealing with the activities of foreign companies in the country. Companies already doing business in Korea and those approaching Korea in the future will invariably encounter *chakupjachok* in some way, and should prepare for it.

In the future self-sufficiency will continue to be an important issue in Korea because Koreans, like other Asians, have long historical memories and are determined to prevent their country from ever again being dependent on or controlled by foreign nations.

Collective Responsibility

Korea's traditional system of Confucian filial piety and "familyism" made it impossible for most of its citizens to develop strong senses of individuality or the ability to act freely on their own.

In this collectivist system there was no such thing as personal *chaegim* (chay-gheem), or "responsibility." Instead of individuals assuming culpability for their own behavior, personal actions were seen as reflections on one's family and families were accordingly held responsible for the behavior of their individual members. This system of social control meant that enforcement of both social and legal codes fell to families—fathers and grand-fathers who, to use a modern concept, played the role of "godfa-thers" in Mafia organizations. Their word was final in virtually all matters.

In contrast with the individualism and self-determination that came to be valued in Western societies, this system encouraged the group-minded approach to life that become the norm in Korea. Decision, activity, and responsibility were the realm of the many, not the few.

The power of this cultural element has now diminished, but enough of it remains to play a fundamental role in Korean life, particularly in business and politics—both of which continue to be viewed as group activities.

The Extraordinary Peace of Mind Factor

A primary theme found in both Buddhism and Confucianism can be subsumed in the Korean term *anshim* (ahn-sheem), or "peace of mind." This become an integral part of the Korean character and was eventually incorporated into both the etiquette and laws of the land.

Anshim called on Koreans to avoid mental chaos, physical violence, and any activity that disrupted the order of their society. It became so pronounced in Korean behavior that ancient Chinese visitors to the peninsula made note of it in their reports. One report famously referred to Korea as "The Land of Morning Calm," implying that life in Korea was as peaceful and calm as an early morning before people began to move about.

For individuals, *anshim* required the suppression of virtu-ally all emotions. The resulting peace and calmness—however superficial it may have been—was the primary impetus for the development of a special skill called *nunchi* (noon-chee), or "face-reading." I define this as "cultural telepathy." It is an extra sense that Koreans must develop to understand the largely unexpressed feelings and intentions of others. Koreans must be able to "read" the faces and minds of the people around them in order to interact with them in a way that recognizes and sustains *anshim* and maintains harmonious relationships. While this kind of cultural intelligence is not unknown in the West, it is not as important or highly developed there.

Another facet of *anshim* in Korean culture is expressed with the words *in'gan kwan'gye* (een-gahn kwahn-gay), which mean "interpersonal relations." Great effort is taken to ensure that interpersonal relationships proceed in ways that ensure peace of mind by not embarrassing or shaming anyone. *In'gan kwan'gye*, often described as one of the most important terms in the Korean language, is used in virtually every definition and explanation of the structure and workings of Korean society.

In addition to these relatively positive influences, *Anshim* also had a negative impact on Korean society by creating an extraordinary divide between people's thoughts and their behavior. Because they had no socially accepted recourse other than keeping their emotions bottled up in this way, individuals sometimes lost control and virtually exploded into verbal or physical violence. Koreans thus developed dual personalities—one personality that epitomized the calm demeanor and behavior taught by Buddhism and Confucianism, and another personality that was marked by fits of extreme violent behavior.

For men this violence was typically physical; for women it was generally verbal, although there were also numerous occasions when women would take direct physical action against those they believed to have wronged them. The propensity for men—especially those who had been drinking—to become violent was so widespread that an early Chosun king issued a decree that they had to wear hats made of heavy ceramic rather than the traditional, light-weight stovepipe hats made of horse-hair. Men who fought vigorously enough to knock these weighty hats from their heads would be severely punished. Naturally, Korean men subsequently developed extraordinary skill at engaging in pubic brawls while keeping their hats balanced on their heads. (As farfetched as it may seem, this practice may be the origin of the old Western saying that hot-tempered people will "fight at the drop of a hat.")

There are fairly frequent outbreaks of institutional and personal violence in Korea that can seem to be shocking departures from normal behavior to those who do not understand *anshim*. The most conspicuous of these ritualized acts of violence involve union members and political groups that become frustrated and resort to violence to get attention and obtain redress.

Anshim continues to influence the daily lives of Koreans in both positive and negative ways. Behavior that may appear to be odd, if not irrational, to Westerners is likely a manifestation of the *anshim* factor in Korean culture.

Feelings Come First

If I had to choose the most important words that influence Korean etiquette, *kibun* (kee-boon) would be near the top of my list. *Kibun* means "feelings" or "sensations" and is the barometer that Koreans use to measure and define virtually every aspect of their lives, including their personal and professional relationships.

This barometer is of course just as commonly used in the Western world when it comes to personal relationships. However, in our business and professional relationships we are obliged—and often required—to suppress our feelings and react rationally and logically on the basis of facts and other objective criteria. In Korea this is generally not the case: the typical Korean reaction in virtually all situations tends to be feelings first, with facts, logic, and rationality second or third. This focus on emotion has traditionally prompted Koreans to protect their own feelings and the feelings of others. This means they never criticize anyone publicly, except in the case of superiors berating subordinates. In addition, they avoid being the bearer of bad news and do everything in their power to maintain a facade of harmony in their relationships.

Foreigners can unknowingly upset the *kibun* of Koreans by behaving in ways that Koreans consider *koman* (kuh-mahn), or arrogant. This happens when foreigners fail to take into account the feelings of Koreans and behave in fact-based, logical, and rational ways, or in ways that could be seen as self-serving.

Kibun is especially important in business situations. Foreign businesspeople should be aware of it and take measures to avoid hurting the *kibun* of employees and others they must deal with.

Feelings as a Refuge and Weapon

Throughout most of its history Korea's hierarchical culture left many people essentially powerless. These people had one recourse—influencing those in power with emotional manipulations that did not directly contravene social customs or government taboos.

Thus *kamjong* (kahm-johng), or "emotions," became both a refuge and a weapon that Koreans used to get their way in situations outside the bounds of their strict etiquette. Women in particular used emotion to influence men in personal matters.

The power of emotions impacted the structure and function of Korean society on every level. Until the second half of the twentieth century personal ties based on *kamjong* took precedence over virtually everything in the lives of Koreans. These personal connections ensured the safety that was not guaranteed by individual human rights or a body of impartial law.

Although both human rights and rule by law now thrive in Korea, feelings, not rational thought, remain the basis for the overwhelming majority of Korean behavior and attitudes.

The sea of emotion in which Koreans live can be and often is very upsetting to logic- and fact-minded Westerners, who tend to regard many forms of Korean behavior as both irrational and counterproductive.

The Cosmic Force Is with Them!

Another important cultural element in Korea is unique to the Chinese sphere of Asia. It is subsumed in the term *ki* (kee), which refers to the ancient Chinese concept of a cosmic force that empowers and exists within all life in the universe. *Ki* might be described as the Asian counterpart to Western God-based religions.

While the attempted manipulation of *ki* in modern Korea is generally limited to practitioners of the martial arts, belief in this concept is integrated into Korean culture. It is notably reflected in the energy and passion Koreans bring to their work and their reaction to nature.

Koreans believe that rivers and mountains in particular are imbued with *ki*, and regard them to be sacred. Many of Korea's greatest shrines and temples are built on or near mountain summits and each year millions of Korean go on ritualistic pilgrimages to mountains. The most sacred mountain on the Korean peninsula is Diamond Mountain in North Korea. (In the 1990s the North Korean government began allowing South Koreans to visit the mountain on tightly controlled—and expensive!—group tours.)

Koreans generally do not discuss the concept or use of *ki* in their lives but they attribute much of their strength, vitality, and extraordinary economic success to its power.

How Koreans View Foreigners

Koreans place foreigners in two basic categories—those who are in Korea for short periods of time as visitors, and those who are there as long term residents.

Tourists are treated as guests and therefore receive a high level of hospitality. Koreans take great pride in showing off their culture and the beauty of their homeland, and they welcome visitors wholeheartedly.

Resident foreigners are a different matter. Once their status is recognized as something other than that of visitor, they do not automatically qualify for treatment as guests. The general population treats them as strangers to whom they have no ties and no obligations—just as they treat other Koreans they do not know. These long-term residents, like strangers, are treated with courtesy and respect as long as they themselves behave with decorum.

One of the biggest factors influencing the reaction to foreigners living and working in Korea is whether these foreigners are fluent in Korea's language and culture. Foreigners often do not know precisely what is going on, what is said, what is expected of them, or how to react in an appropriate manner. Koreans find this understandably off-putting. This is compounded by the fact that a great deal of person-to-person communication in Korea is nonverbal or expressed in ways that are not comprehensible to the typical foreign newcomer. This situation can be irritating but is something that foreigners have to live with until they become fluent in both Korea's language and nonverbal culture.

Another thing that impacts all foreigners who spend lengthy periods of time in Korea—including living there full-time for life—is that they will always be seen as foreigners: Korean ethnicity is exclusive to Koreans. Although foreigners are generally treated kindly and with respect, they almost always remain outside the pale of Korean society.

The Religion Factor in Korea

Some 40 percent of South Koreans profess a religious affiliation. That affiliation is spread among a great variety of traditions, including Buddhism (34 percent), Christianity (21 percent), Confucianism (0.2 percent), and shamanism. But in truth most of these numbers are meaningless because there are few if any distinctions between believers and nonbelievers in Buddhism and Confucianism, and virtually all Koreans follow some shamanistic practices.

There is also a small Muslim minority in Korea. A number of newer religions have adherents there as well, but they have very little if any impact on the country as a whole.

With the exception of Christianity, religions do not play a conspicuous role in the daily lives of the people of Korea. The various religious activities that do take place are more form than substance. Aspects of both Buddhism and Confucianism, for example, are sometimes so deeply embedded in the mindset and behavior of Koreans today that they constitute a lifestyle rather than a religious belief.

Companies and other organizations routinely call in Buddhist priests to bless new buildings and new enterprises. But again, the religious significance of these practices does not go much beyond the rituals.

Many Koreans attend or participate in shamanism-based festivals on one or more occasions each year, but for the majority these events are more like entertainment than religious rituals. Large numbers of Koreans also visit Buddhist temples, usually on family outings, where they bow and leave offerings.

Foreign visitors in Korea do not have to learn or follow any special protocol when visiting Buddhist temples. They should simply be polite to any priests they may encounter, stay out of areas that are not open to the public, avoid being loud and rowdy, and in general behave in a respectful manner.

Ordinary visitors to Buddhist temples do not go "inside" the inner sanctums of the temples. Instead, they walk around outside, admiring the architecture of the buildings and the images of deities that are enshrined in the temples and visible from the public areas.

Part II

Personal Etiquette in Korea Today

Traditionally the rules of etiquette in Korea were dependent on gender, age, personal relationship, social class, and professional rank. All of these factors continue to play a role in the day-to-day behavior of Koreans, but they are far less significant than they were and are becoming less important among younger generations with each passing year.

In addition to the members of these younger generations—whose behavior is not that different from what passes as good etiquette in the United States and other Western countries—there is a large and growing community of Koreans who behave very much like Westerners when dealing with them.

While there are still key areas of behavior and rules that visitors and businesspeople should know about and follow while interacting with Koreans, Koreans do not expect foreign visitors or residents to know and precisely follow all of the current rules of etiquette that are unique to their country.

However, understanding the distinct attributes of Korean etiquette can make a visit to Korea—or a long-term stay there—far more rewarding.

Family Names

An important aspect of social etiquette that persists in Korea is the role and significance of family names, given names, relationship designations, and titles.

The total number of family names in Korea may be a factor in their importance. In contrast with Europe—where cultures were much less cohesive, people's histories were shorter, and where people historically took or were given names based on the work they did, where they lived, and so on—surnames in Korea have been more or less limited to those of Korea's original founding clans.

As time passed, the names of these first families became semi-sacred. A law was even passed that prohibited common people who could not trace their ancestry to the founding families from having or using a family name, a right members of these clans reserved for themselves. This law was not rescinded for males until the late 1800s, and it was 1909 before female commoners could take family names. To this day an almost mystic aura surrounds the ancient names—a factor that makes Koreans very sensitive about their family names and their use.

There are now only about 300 *song* (sohng), or family names, in all of Korea. Approximately half of all Koreans are named Kim, Lee, Choi, or Pak. According to Korean population statistics 21.7 percent of all Koreans are named Kim, 14.8 percent are named Lee (also written as Yi and Rhee), and 8.5 percent are named Pak (also written as Park). The next seven most common family names are Choe (Chay), Chung, Kang, Cho, Yun, Chang (Jang), and Rim (Rheem). Altogether, these 10 names account for about 65 percent of the population.

From the earliest times, this limited number of family names presented Koreans with a major challenge. Identifying and keeping track of even close relatives, much less people at large, was not something that could be taken lightly. This problem was remedied by informally and arbitrarily adding a number of additional bits and pieces of information to each name—such as the individual's address, workplace, title, and so on.

Not surprisingly, the name situation was particularly challenging when the first Westerners took up residence in Korea after the 1870s—and it is now even more difficult because the population is more than 10 times larger than what it was then. Today the problem is mitigated somewhat by businesspeople and others having name cards. Nonetheless, both short-term foreign visitors and resident foreigners must make a point of gathering enough additional information about each of the Kims, Lees, and others they meet that they can include these details in any reference to the individuals.

For example, in a single large organization today there are often as many as a thousand people named Kim and Lee. And since it has traditionally been taboo among adult Koreans to refer to others by their given names, a custom that is still generally followed, this makes it imperative that you identify the Kim or Lee or Park to whom you are referring with his or her title, section, division, and so on.

This difficulty in distinguishing between those with the same family name has traditionally caused Koreans to avoid calling people by name. Instead, they used titles, positions, trades, professions, scholastic ranks, or some honorific, such as *teacher*. Parents were typically addressed as the equivalent of "Jimmy's mommy" or "Susie's daddy," rather than "Mrs. Kim" or "Mr. Kim."

If you do not know someone's title and your relationship to him or her is unclear, you should use the generic Korean honorific when speaking to him or her. This is *sshi* (sshe)—"Kim Sshi," "Lee Sshi," and so on. (In the Korean government system of Romanizing the language, this title is spelled *ssi*.)

Married women in Korea do not take their husbands' surnames and are called by their maiden name and the honorific Mrs. when addressed directly (for example, Mrs. Kim). When referred to indirectly they are identified as the wife of Mr. Lee or Mr. Choe, and so on. There are other ways of addressing and referring to wives, but using the English honorific *Mrs.* is fine.

It is also perfectly acceptable to use the English terms Mr. and Miss when referring to men and single women. Virtually all Koreans know and understand these English words.

Family names are placed first by Koreans when writing or speaking, with given names following after.

Given Names

Early in their history Koreans adopted the Chinese custom of having two given names. One was referred to as a "generational name," and was given in honor of an illustrious ancestor; the other was a given name that embodied some character trait parents wanted their child to have. Each of these names has traditionally been written with a single *hantcha*, or Chinese character.

Now some Korean families register the names of their children in the native Korean script, *hangul*, rather than *hantcha*. When the two given names are written with Roman letters they may be spelled as one word or a hyphen may be inserted between them, which is a matter of personal preference.

Some Korean families that belong to younger generations now give their children only one name. In some cases they choose a foreign name, assuming that it will benefit the child in a work environment.

Within families, children generally do not address older family members by their given names. For example, a girl addresses her older brother as *oppa* (op-pah) and her older sister as *onni* (own-nee); a boy addresses his older brother as *hyung* (hyuung) and his older sister as *nuna* (nuu-nah). Both boys and girls may address younger brothers and sisters using their given names.

In spite of traditional taboos, more and more friends and members of the younger generations are beginning to call each other by their given names. Especially in the international community, it is also common for men (but so far not for women) to use only the initials of their two given names to make it easier for foreigners to deal with them.

Age and Etiquette

It is common for Koreans to ask new acquaintances their age shortly after meeting them in social situations, because age is a crucial factor in determining hierarchy. Young people in particular consider individuals who are the same age to be part of the same peer group, allowing them to dispense with the more formal terms of respect discussed above. Also, it allows them to be more casual in their demeanor.

There are now etiquette advisors who say that if you are fewer than 10 years younger than someone you may consider yourself their peer and act accordingly. I would not suggest doing so until you have become well acquainted with the individual concerned—except, perhaps, in purely social settings.

Bow or Shake Hands?

Shaking hands has been widely adopted in Korea, especially among the young and those involved in international affairs. When you shake hands with a senior person for the first time, combining a handshake with a very slight bow is a courteous thing to do.

The *chol* (choll) or bow, a key element in Korean etiquette since ancient times, is still an important part of behavior today. Among themselves Koreans still do a great deal of bowing. As a Westerner, you will also find bowing to be useful when you are introduced to several people and it is inconvenient or impractical to shake hands with each one. Group bowing at formal meetings is common.

Knowing just how deeply to bow requires an understanding of Korean culture. The deeper the bow, the more humility, respect, sorrow, or gratitude it indicates. The loftier the status of the higher ranking individual, the shallower his or her bow will be when it is not acting as an apology. Generally, superiors do little more than nod their heads to younger staff members, while younger people of lower status determine the degree of their bow on a situation-by-situation basis. If they want something or are in trouble, they will bow deeply and hold that bow longer. Another important rule of bowing etiquette is that the person of lower status is expected to bow first.

Bowing excessively for the situation and the individuals involved puts a different slant on the action. It means you are culturally inept or are attempting to ingratiate yourself for some reason. On the other hand, not bowing low enough to meet the standards of etiquette can also be damaging.

Bowing is also useful when no one immediately responds to you when you enter an office or shop, even if they've seen you. You can indicate you want to speak to someone by bowing toward him or her with an expectant look on your face. You may need to do this, as Koreans can be reluctant to respond immediately to the sudden appearance of a foreigner because they assume that the foreigner does not speak Korean and won't be able communicate successfully.

Foreign businesspeople and visitors to Korea do not need to get hung up on when and how to bow. Koreans don't expect foreigners to bow, but when they do bow—and do so properly— Koreans appreciate it as a demonstration of knowledge and respect for their culture.

Body Language

Your instincts for what is good behavior will serve you well in Korea, but it is nonetheless important for foreign visitors to understand some specific differences between Korean and Western body language.

For example, Koreans usually smile or laugh when they are embarrassed or don't understand something. Although your initial reaction to such behavior may be to think that your Korean contact has found something funny when there was no intent to be humorous, the situation may call for an apology and further explanation.

Also, Koreans traditionally use both hands when receiving something from a person of senior age or rank, or when handing something to a senior individual. This custom is still common in formal situations, especially among women, but like other old Confucian-oriented traditions it is gradually disappearing.

The American custom of beckoning someone by curling and uncurling one's index finger is considered rude in Korea. Instead, Koreans beckon service workers, workmen, and friends by partly extending the right hand in front of their body and waving it up and down in a gesture similar to a wave goodbye. This gesture should not be used when dealing with people with whom you do not have a direct service relationship or friendship.

Another issue to note is that when sitting with your legs and feet exposed in formal and semiformal situations, crossing your legs or pointing your feet at someone were traditionally thought to be rude. (However, fewer and fewer members of the younger generations are holding to this old rule.)

It is also considered rude to conspicuously blow your nose when you are near or facing someone. The accepted etiquette is to turn or step aside. During winter months many Koreans also wear surgical masks over their mouths and noses when out in public. These people have colds and are simply trying to avoid spreading their germs around.

Westerners may be surprised to see Koreans friends of the same sex demonstrating affection for one another in public. They may walk hand-in-hand or hold arms, frequently touch one another, or dance together at clubs and parties.

However, demonstrations of sexual behavior in public, such as kissing, are still rare and considered improper by older Koreans. But given the power of popular culture to change traditional mindsets in only a few short years, this attitude may be gone in no time—even in Korea.

Yes and *No* in Korea

Koreans rarely express a negative response with a blunt *no*. Instead, they may say, "It will be difficult," "We will think about it," or "Maybe"—all responses designed to avoid hurting anyone's feelings. Likewise, Koreans are reluctant to say *yes* in unequivocal terms because they are aware that conditions invariably change.

Koreans also won't typically admit that they do not know the answer when asked a question, which is an automatic response designed to avoid losing face. You should not be unduly upset if you ask someone a question and don't get a truthful reply or get no reply at all; in such cases it is often possible to rephrase your question so that the person can give you a truthful response without losing face.

Apologizing Saves the Day

Korea's traditionally strict etiquette system, enforced by harsh social as well as government sanctions, resulted in people becoming exceedingly sensitive to even minor slips in the prescribed code of behavior. This made *sagwa* (sah-gwah), or an apology, a virtually instinctive response to any situation, including ones that might have seemed minor by Western standards. This prominence of the apology is rooted in a belief that it's better to apologize when an apology isn't really called for than it is to take a chance that you might offend someone.

Frequent apologies continue to be part of Korean behavior, and it is considered polite to apologize in advance for the possibility that you might impose on other people or unknowingly commit some kind of offense.

It is also customary for lectures and speeches to begin with an apology rather than the Western practice of beginning them with jokes. (My approach has been to apologize for not having an appropriate joke!)

Red-carpet Hospitality

Koreans are famous for their *hwandae* (hwahn-die), or hospitality, which can be so aggressive and sumptuous that people who are not used to it may feel overwhelmed. Conspicuous hospitality is a distinguishing characteristic of Koreans in both private and business settings, but corporate hospitality is generally even more extravagant than private hospitality.

There are several reasons for the Korean emphasis on hospitality. In part, this custom derived from Korea's native shamanistic folk religion, which incorporated a strong concept of sharing. The influences of Buddhism and Confucianism also impacted the importance of hospitality in Korean society: Buddhism taught magnanimity and Confucianism required a communal attitude toward material things. Another major factor was hospitality's role in building up favors or obligations that its recipients were expected to return in the future. Also, it gave the hosts face.

Today hospitality in Korea can even be something of a competitive sport. Especially when foreign visitors are hosting social or business events, it is common for Korean guests to grab the check away from their host with the intention of paying it. It goes without saying that this should not be allowed; instead, the host should slip away from the party a few minutes before it ends to pay the bill in advance. Otherwise, the delivery of the bill can result in a wrestling match that might become lively.

In the past it was customary for the senior person in a group to pay restaurant bills. This is still the custom in many personal and private situations. However, younger people and coworkers who go to restaurants together for lunch or dinner generally pay their own bills.

Tipping in Korea

The Western custom of tipping waiters, taxi drivers, bellhops, and other service workers is growing in popularity in Korea. This is particularly true at international hotels, first-class restaurants that cater to foreign clientele, barber shops, and hostess nightclubs. Some upscale restaurants add a surcharge to their bills that is supposed to take the place of tipping. Businesses may also post "no tipping" signs. Rather than perhaps offending someone by either tipping or not tipping, it is best to ask if tipping is expected or allowed.

Dining Etiquette

In the past a variety of involved dining customs and rules were followed by most Koreans in their homes and in public places, but dining etiquette is now much more informal. Koreans do not expect foreigners to behave in the traditional Korean manner, and will often guide and advise guests on seating arrangements and dining customs. As a guest, all you have to do when dining with a Korean host is wait courteously and follow the instructions you are given.

In Korean-style restaurants and homes diners sit on the floor and eat off low tables designed for this use. Many Korean restaurants have private rooms in addition to communal dining areas that are booth- or alcove-like. These private rooms are normally used by small to large groups.

Traditional Korean dining etiquette is slightly different from what Westerners may be used to. If the only way you can get the last bit of soup is by picking up your soup bowl and drinking from it, go ahead and do so. Rather than being a display of bad manners this just shows you like the soup. (You might smile when doing it as a gesture to an old formality.) On the other hand, you should not poke chopsticks upright into a bowl of rice and leave them there because this traditionally signified that the original user of the chopsticks had died. And when using a toothpick, cover your mouth with your free hand. Not doing this is considered rude (if not uncivilized).

Don't think it strange if older Koreans are quiet at the dinner table. Unlike Chinese, Americans, and people from many other

cultures who engage in loud, nonstop conversations while dining, older Koreans are generally quiet when eating. (But not so
the younger generations!) Also, it is an old Korean custom to
wait for the oldest person at the table to begin eating first. When
dining with guests, Korean hosts can sometimes also be aggressive in insisting that their guests start eating first.

During traditional Korean meals several different dishes are
likely to be served, and individuals can help themselves from
platters placed family-style in the center of the table. Each person will have his or her own bowl of rice.

Korean dishes are generally eaten with either chopsticks or
heavy ceramic spoons, which are used for soup and rice dishes.
Restaurants that are accustomed to serving foreigners may
provide Western-style knives and forks in their table settings or
have some available by request.

Restaurants, both Western- and Korean-style, are abundant
in Korea. They range from street vendors (*pojangmacha*/poh-
jahng-mah-chah) and small restaurants (*shikdang*/sheek-dahng)
to upscale places with fancy full-course meals and prices to
match. Tea and coffee shops abound, along with bars, pubs,
upscale clubs, and rock cafes that also serve food.

When visiting Korea, it pays to know something about the
most common Korean dishes. You will have to make choices of
your own while out on the town, and perhaps also while visiting
someone's home. Here are some of the most common dishes.

Chap chae (chop chay). This is a mixture of clear noodles
and a variety of diced vegetables and meat.

Naeng myun (nang m'yuun). A summer dish consisting
of buckwheat noodles served cold either with or without
beef broth. It is served with strips of beef, half a hard-
boiled egg, and vegetables.

Kim (keem). Seaweed that is sometimes wrapped around vegetables and seasoned rice to make *kim bap* (keem bahp), a common picnic food.

Mandoo (mahn-doo). Small dumplings filled with vegetables and meat that are served in a hot soup, fried, or steamed.

Bee bim bap (bee beem bahp). A large bowl of rice covered with vegetables served with a lightly cooked egg on the side that the diner stirs into the mix.

Bulgogi (buhl-go-ghee). Thin strips of beef that have been marinated in soy sauce, garlic, green onions, and sugar, then barbecued, usually on a metal grill built into your table. This dish is generally reserved for special occasions.

Kalbi (kahl-bee). Barbecued beef ribs prepared in a way similar to *bulgogi*.

Kalbi chim (kahl-bee cheem). A seasoned beef-rib casserole served with simmered carrots, mushrooms, chestnuts, and potatoes.

Yak gwa (yahk gwah). A fried biscuit made with honey, ginger, sesame oil, and pine nuts. It is orange or brown and usually shaped like a flower.

Kimchi (kee-chee). Synonymous with Korean dining, this spicy hot pickled cabbage dish is a part of virtually every meal. In restaurants you can sometimes request mild or extra hot versions.

Drinking Etiquette

The drinking of alcoholic beverages plays a major role in interpersonal and business relationships in Korea. It is also far more institutionalized and ritualized than in most countries other than China and Japan, where drinking is common for the same reasons it is common in Korea.

To cope with Korea's Confucian-based morality and etiquette it became culturally acceptable for Koreans to let their hair down while they were drinking alcohol, allowing them to say and do things that were taboo in other situations. Naturally this led drinking to become a regular part of life in Korea—for men, at least. They drank to relieve the stress of conforming to strict etiquette, to give their emotions free rein, and to really get to know each other.

Today drinking is a major social and business pastime in Korea for the same reasons. It has become so deeply ingrained in the culture that Koreans continue to do it even as pressure from traditional etiquette is on the wane.

There is considerable pressure to drink; Korean hosts are typically aggressive in pushing drinks on visitors and resident businesspeople. If you don't drink, you can lessen the pressure to do so by explaining this before the party begins. The most acceptable reason for not drinking is a health problem that prevents you from doing so: those who are under strict orders from medical professionals not to consume alcohol will not be pressured to drink. In strictly social or diplomatic situations you can usually get by with ordering a soft drink so that you can participate in the inevitable toasts.

As time passes, pressure to drink is becoming less of an issue. As Korean lifestyles have become more and more international-ized and the pressure to maintain a high level of performance has grown to stratospheric levels, there is less and less pressure to over-drink. Reasons for not overindulging are becoming more acceptable.

But even today a night out on the town with Korean hosts is often filled with drinking rituals. One of this is the traditional *konbae* (kuun-bye) toast, also spelled *gunbae* (guun-bye) or *ganbae* (gahn-bye), which more or less means "Bottoms Up!"

Many people also still follow the old drinking ritual that involves handing guests at parties empty glasses, filling these glasses, and watching while the partygoers drink them down. This ritual is then reversed.

It has also long been established etiquette for people to make a point of pouring drinks for their seniors, making sure that their glasses are always full even if they just drink in small sips. Sometimes younger members of a group will actually line up to fill your glass and toast with you to demonstrate their sincerity and goodwill. Seniors may honor juniors by pouring drinks for them. Old etiquette for this situation required the juniors to receive these glasses with both hands and turn aside when drinking.

In the old days, pourers would cup the right-hand sleeves of their flowing garments with their left hands to keep them from interfering with the pouring.

A very important point to keep in mind in all drinking situations in Korea is that when you empty your glass completely it is a sign that you want a refill. More often than not someone will refill your empty glass to the brim.

If you wish to drink lightly, you must be firm on this point and only sip your drink no matter how many times it is refilled or how aggressive people are in refilling it. Some might also recommend feigning a degree of drunkenness you don't feel in order to keep up with the crowd and to prevent yourself from loosing face or making others feel uncomfortable, which would inhibit their behavior.

If you do overindulge, never fear. Koreans have come up with a "cure" for hangovers. Called *baejangguk* (by-jahng-guuk), this is a beef-bone broth fortified with the dried outer leaves of cabbage and clotted ox blood. Some drinking places used to serve this concoction to heavy drinkers at the end of a night of drinking. Now it is mostly a morning-after drink, and it may not be readily available unless you know where to go!

In Korea, alcohol is its own kind of tradition. It is so important that two drinks have been designated Important Intangible Cultural Properties by the government. One is a liquor called *munbaeju* (muun-by-juu), which is distilled from wheat and millet and has the scent and flavor of crabapple. (*Munbae* means "crabapple.") The other is an azalea wine called *dugyeonju* (duug-yohn-juu).

Korea's "national drink," *soju* (soh-juu), is the equivalent of Japan's famous sake (sah-kay). It is comparable to vodka, but less potent. While originally brewed from rice and other grains, today *soju* is usually distilled from sweet potatoes.

Virtually every region in Korea has its own traditional liquors and wines that have long been famous and are popular among travelers as gift items. Some of these drinks are brewed from grains and fruits. Two of the more common ones are *makgolli* (mahk-gohl-lee) and *dongdongju* (dong-dong-juu), milky liquors with low alcohol content that were originally the drinks of farmers and laborers, but have since gone upscale. They are now served in pubs near universities and office buildings, at festivals and picnics, and on other occasions when someone wants a mild drink with a fermented flavor.

The side dishes or snacks that generally go with drinking in Korea are known as *anju* (ahn-juu), and include nuts, mung beans, and dried beef, fish, or octopus. Some upscale places have *anju* menus, but these tidbits are generally served whether you order them or not and are added to your bill.

Home Invitations

Koreans have a long history of inviting *sonnim* (sohn-neem), or guests, into their homes. Historically the front part of homes belonging to the more well-to-do even included special rooms where male members of the family spent much of their free time entertaining guests with sumptuous meals and alcoholic beverages. When democratic principles and equal rights for women were introduced into the country in the mid 1950s, the tradition of entertaining guests in one's home was automatically extended to women.

Today Koreans take considerable pleasure and pride in extending *chodae* (choh-dic), or invitations, to their friends, both foreign and Korean. This custom plays an important role in society, and Koreans typically explain that foreigners who really want to understand them must learn the word *chodae*—and all that it means to Koreans.

The commonality of home visits, which are far more revealing and intimate than meetings at restaurants or bars, is one of the reasons why it is easier and faster to develop close relationships with Koreans than with Japanese and other Asians. Foreign residents in Korea can take advantage of this aspect of Korean culture by inviting Korean friends and contacts to their homes. The benefits are quick and lasting.

The meals served at these gatherings are conspicuous for both the variety of dishes and the volume of food. In fact, a traditional aspect of home visits was that more affluent families would periodically invite less fortunate relatives to their homes for meals, allowing them to take large helpings of leftovers home with them.

The protocol for visiting Korean homes for lunch or dinner is not unusual and requires no special training. It is always appropriate to bring a gift, especially if you are invited for dinner. A bottle of wine or a neatly wrapped package of bakery products can fulfill this requirement of Korean etiquette.

You should wear clean and unholy stockings or socks when visiting a Korean home because you will probably be required to take your shoes off in the entrance foyer. Koreans (like Japanese) think that wearing street shoes in a house with carpeted or fragile-matted floors is cavemanlike. Sit where you are told to sit, be polite, don't get so drunk you can't control yourself, try all of the dishes served, don't stay too long after the meal, and thank your host graciously.

Korean hosts consider it a courtesy to accompany departing guests to the gate (if their home is enclosed in a yard, as many are) or to their car, waving and bowing as they leave. In business situations it is customary to accompany visitors of any rank to the elevator and push the down button for them, or to accompany them to the front of the building if they are important or high-ranking.

Sitting on the Floor

In traditional Korean restaurants and homes diners sit on the floor. This can cause problems for people who are unaccustomed to doing so, or those who are elderly or heavy. It can also be a challenge for women wearing short or tight skirts. These factors should be taken into consideration in choosing where to dine and what to wear.

Some Korean-style restaurants and homes have "floor chairs" to make sitting on the floor more comfortable. These are chairs without legs that are designed to serve as backrests.

Beware of Hot Floors!

While sitting on the floor in Korean homes, Westerners may notice a peculiar problem: overheating. Long ago Koreans adapted an ancient Chinese method of heating their homes and buildings that was apparently the world's first central heating system. They funneled the heat from their cooking stoves and fireplaces beneath the floors, providing a kind of radiant heat that was more effective than systems used in many of the world's most advanced countries today.

This system, known as *ondol* (awn-dohl), is still used in homes as well as in multi-storied and high-rise buildings in Korea, where hot water is circulated through pipes built into the floors. In frigid Korean winters this method of heating can make the floors toasty warm and very comfortable places to sit and sleep. However, in some instances the floors may get so hot that you must be careful about touching them with your bare hands or bottom. This also means that fragile things likely to melt or be damaged by heat should not be placed directly on the floor.

Historians say that the traditional flowing *hanbok* (hahn-bohk) attire was designed with hot floors in mind. The women's version of the *hanbok* in particular tends to form a "tent" around the individual, trapping the heat radiating up from the floor.

Korean Culture in Action

Visitors and foreign residents who are especially interested in Korean culture would be well advised to attend one or more performances at the National Theater of Korea in Seoul. There you can see, hear, and feel Korea's traditional culture in action and gain an understanding of the principles and values that are still very much alive in the minds of modern Koreans.

One of the most remarkable offerings at the National Theater was a musical entitled *The Last Empress* that depicted the life and times of Queen Min, the final empress of the Chosun Dynasty (1392–1910). Over 10 years, 660 performances of it were staged in the National Theater, and it won rave reviews during runs in New York and London.

Electronic Etiquette

Korea is one of the most electronically wired countries in the world, and by 2002 this was reflected in the vast amount of e-mail spam that was originating in the country. This led the Korean Information Security Agency (KISA) to pass legislation designed to control mass unsolicited e-mail by imposing heavy fines and blocking e-mails from some servers.

But the use of e-mail by younger Koreans had already peaked by the turn of the millennium. Young people dropped e-mail in favor of other technologies such as instant messaging, mini–home pages, and text messaging through short message services (SMS). In 2003 alone the total number of monthly e-mail messages on the largest carriers dropped by approximately one billion, while both mini–home page and SMS use skyrocketed.

Polls conducted in 2003 among Korean teens and people in their 20s revealed that members of the younger generations were turned off by e-mail because the process was "too slow and too impersonal." Some said they never used e-mail; others said they used it only when e-mailing older people who did not use messaging services.

Korea has very strict laws regarding e-mail content. Senders of commercial e-mails containing obscene, drug-related, or graphically violent material are subject to prison terms and high fines. Harvesting e-mail addresses from the Internet is also prohibited.

However, according to government reports some 85 percent of the registered Internet users in Korea, including individuals and businesses of all sizes, have multiple e-mail accounts, some of which are obviously used for business purposes.

The use of English-language e-mail in Korea's business community is relatively small but of growing importance, as the number of Koreans who read and write English increases. Those who do use and respond to e-mail messages use the same form of address and salutations that are used in old-fashioned letters.

Korean etiquette about the use of cell phones and other personal electronic devices in public is similar to that in Japan, the United States, and other countries where users are asked to refrain from disturbing other people, particularly on subways and in libraries, movie theaters, and other places where quiet and decorum are expected.

Wedding Celebrations

Visitors to Korea invariably encounter wedding parties in the international hotels where they are staying. This presents them with an opportunity to view modern-day Korean culture in all of its finery and to witness some of the extraordinary changes that have occurred in Korea since the mid twentieth century.

During the long Chosun Dynasty marriages were arranged and wedding ceremonies were long, drawn-out ritualistic affairs. Girls were usually married between the ages of 12 and 16, and grooms in upper-class families were often two or three years younger than their brides. In rural areas grooms were generally two or three years older than their brides.

Following the introduction of democracy in Korea *yeonae* (yoh-nie), or "love marriages," rapidly grew more common. Now both love marriages and *jungmae* (juung-my), or arranged marriages, are common, and couples are typically in their mid or late twenties when they marry.

Most marriage go-betweens, both professionals and friends or family members acting in this role, still follow traditions such as consulting fortune-tellers to make sure a potential bride and groom have enough in common for a harmonious marriage.

Nowadays weddings for ordinary folk are usually held in public halls and churches, while middle- and upper-class families hold weddings in international hotel chapels and ballrooms. Wedding attire is often mixed, with the groom dressed in the Western style and the bride in traditional Korean dress. Guests normally wear Western attire.

Weddings are followed by elaborate receptions, after which couples go on honeymoons, often to overseas destinations.

Start-life-over Parties

It has long been the custom for Koreans to mark their *hwan-gap* (hwahn-gop), or 60th birthday, with a grand banquet party involving family members, relatives, and close friends.

Family members and friends invited to these birthday celebrations bring gifts, including money in white envelopes. During these parties the honoree's sons and daughters bow to him or her, and then other family members and guests do the same. Start-life-over parties sometimes feature live entertainment and also typically include singing, dancing, and impromptu skits. And, of course, there are speeches.

In earlier times *hwan-gap* was especially significant because so few people reached this advanced age. After this milestone individuals traditionally retired from daily work and started their lives over. Like children, they were free from all mundane responsibilities. They did not, however, lose the authority their senior years afforded them and continued to control and direct the affairs of their families—especially ensuring that their grandchildren were educated and trained in proper etiquette.

Because people now routinely live longer and they choose to remain active during their 60s, these elaborate celebrations are now more likely to occur on an individual's 70th birthday. The 70th birthday party is known as *gohui* (go-whee), which means "old and rare."

Count yourself honored if you are invited to a *hwan-gap* or *gohui*.

The Special Role of Gift Giving

Formal and informal gift giving has traditionally played a vital role in the lives of Koreans because it served to create obligation and reciprocity between people. But today Koreans also often give gifts simply because they are inherently hospitable and generous.

Although the giving of gifts in Korea tends to be more common, more structured, and more formal than in America, the rules of gift giving and receiving are not that different from those in other countries. Koreans take gifts when invited into others' homes; when they attend weddings, birthday parties, and other celebrations; when attending funerals; and when they go on trips they bring back gifts for family members and friends.

Money is given in special white envelopes at weddings, funerals, and on other occasions. Foreigners attending a Korean wedding may be surprised by the sight of guests standing in line near the door, handing envelopes containing money to someone at a table who is taking names. In Korea this is a natural part of celebrations. At weddings, for example, attendees give money as a gift to defray the cost of the wedding and help the couple set up housekeeping.

Along with money, people also include a note of congratulation and write their names and addresses on the outside of the envelopes. There is no predetermined amount that should be given: this depends on your own financial circumstances and how well you know the individuals getting married. The amounts range from a hundred dollars to a few thousand dollars.

Money given in this way is called *gyolhon chuguigeum* (g'yohlhoon chuu-gwee-guum), or "wedding congratulatory money." The practice originated with the old tradition of people helping each other put on weddings, since the events tend to be elaborate and expensive.

Some people give wedding presents instead of money. In this case, the presents are delivered directly to the home of the new couple.

But gifts are not only given for major events like weddings; they're also part of day-to-day life. When traveling abroad Koreans take small gifts to give to business contacts and people who help them or extend hospitality to them. This is a custom that others can easily adopt if they don't already do it.

Generally Koreans do not open gifts as soon as they receive them, and will do so only when urged on by the giver. The quality of gift packaging—the wrapping paper, box, and so on—is virtually as important to Koreans as the gift itself. The more refined and the higher the quality a gift's packaging, the more face there is to be had in giving or receiving it.

A bit of common sense is all that is needed to decide what to give. The gift that one chooses to give should be based on its intended recipient—a child, a young boy or girl, a young woman, a businessperson, and so on. Like most everyone else Koreans appreciate gifts that have cultural value, particularly ones that are famous products associated with gift-giver's home area or the area the gift itself came from.

There are some old taboos about gift giving that are studiously listed in guidebooks—some of which are still valid. However some of these warnings are nonsense, such as ones that advise against giving knives or scissors because of their cutting implications. And anyone who advises against giving liquor to women apparently doesn't know very many modern-day Korean women.

There are a few pointers to keep in mind when giving gifts in Korea: Giving gifts in multiples of four is taboo because the word for four is pronounced like the word for death. Seven is a lucky number. Red or yellow wrapping paper is appropriate, as these were royal colors, and pink wrapping paper is also acceptable. Cards should never be signed in red ink, which in this case signifies death.

The Skill of Bargaining

Foreigners who shop or engage in business in Korea should be aware of the country's tradition of bargaining. As in all old societies bargaining in Korea has been an important economic skill and, like most people, Koreans also see bargaining as a social skill.

Until recent times there were no widely established principles for setting the cost of goods or the value of labor, which caused the development and widespread use of bargaining. Today Korean department stores, fine boutiques, and upscale institutions have fixed prices. But in the great city markets, *enuri* (eh-nuu-ree) or haggling, to use a colloquial term, is still practiced by merchants and shoppers. (However, a word of warning where brand-name foreign products such as watches are concerned—if the tagged price is already especially low and the vendor still agrees to a significant discount, there is a real possibility that the item is a fake.)

Korean bargaining sessions can be loud affairs, and although they are mostly good-natured they may sound like fights to the uninformed. There is a phrase for this kind of display: *chugoni-batkoni* (chuu-goh-nee baht-koh-nee), meaning "give-and-take."

There is something else visitors should know about bargaining and negotiating in Korea. The typical Korean is a master at bargaining: The nature of their class- and rank-based society has made it imperative for Koreans to develop considerable verbal skills and to become especially clever at using emotional tactics in their bargaining. The latter typically throws Westerners for a loop because they have little or no experience in using emotion as a bargaining tool.

In contrast, Koreans sometimes turn the negotiation of simple points into high drama by the introduction various emotional elements. When this happens, remain calm and collected and stick to your guns until your Korean counterpart accepts your position.

Clothing Matters!

Koreans rank among the world's best-dressed people. Korean women take great pride in being fashionably dressed, and Korean men, as some wag noted years ago, were born wearing suits and ties.

Koreans are concerned about their apparel for deep-seated cultural reasons. For millennia Koreans' social statuses were evident from the clothing they wore, and misreading this often had serious consequences because an individual's status determined to a great extent the kind and level of etiquette required when interacting with him her or her. This prompted Koreans to be acutely attuned to what people wore. Today this attention to sartorial detail is still very much in evidence.

Although Western-style dress is now the norm, many Koreans wear traditional *hanbok* on special days such as the lunar New Year; *Chuseok* (Chuu-soak), or "Thanksgiving"; and family festivities such as *hwan-gap*, the 60th birthday celebration.

Visitors to Korea do not need to go overboard where dressing is concerned. Casual and comfortable clothing is fine for touring and sightseeing, but visitors should keep in mind that if they are going to be staying in first-class hotels, dining in first-class restaurants, and visiting prominent public places the casual dress they wear at home may be conspicuously out of place. This applies especially to young people and in particular to boys and girls who wear clothing that is by Korean standards both unsightly and indecent. This includes baggy trousers and miniskirts.

The Importance of Color

Colors have traditionally been important in Korean culture. Conforming to and appreciating aspects of Korean etiquette requires knowledge of the role that color plays in Korean life.

White, the color of garments traditionally worn by common people, symbolizes modesty and purity of spirit. Red is regarded to be symbolic of good fortune and wealth and was used in women's wedding garments. Indigo, representing steadfastness and loyalty, was used for the skirts of court ladies and the formal coats of court officials. Black, symbolizing infinity and the source of all creation, was used for men's hats. Yellow, which represented the center of the universe, was used for royal garments and could not be worn by common people.

When these five colors were used together they represented the overt virtues of the masculine element in the cosmos. They often appeared in patterns on garments worn above the waist and various combinations of them were used on garments worn by children, in dancing costumes, and for women's purses. Individually, these "Korean" colors were associated with order in the universe.

These colors and all that they represented became deeply ingrained in the mindset of the Korean people. Still today their metaphysical aspects are an important part of Korean culture, and they are integral parts of arts, crafts, decorations, gift-wrapping, and the modernized versions of traditional wearing apparel.

Finding Places on Nameless Streets

One of the challenges that face visitors in Korea is dealing with the country's system of assigning physical addresses, which is very different from the system employed in Western nations.

Korean cities are divided into wards (*gu*), districts (*dong*), and irregularly sized and shaped sections or blocks (*ka*). There are several *dong* in each *gu* and several buildings in each *ka*.

Traditionally, Korean streets did not have names, numbers, or any other kind of official designation. Instead, *chuso* (chuu-soh), or addresses, were based on a series of identifiers that began with a province and descended downward to a ward, a district, a block, and finally a lot within that block. Even today, a typical Korean address is written: Seoul, Choong Gu, Sokong Dong, #87, name of the householder or building. (However, the Korean postal system accepts mail addressed in the Western manner, with the name of the individual or company first.)

For travelers in Korea this system could be problematic because historically buildings within lots were numbered in the order in which they were built, rather than in a sequential way that would indicate their relationships to one another. This made it necessary to have a map to travel to a place for the first time. Without precise aids, finding a location required wandering around within the districts, blocks, and lots until coming across the right address.

Today most major streets in Korea have been named, but place addresses still have nothing to do with the streets they are on or near. (Many have been rationalized so that they are in sequence within their blocks, however.) To help cope with this situation hotels, businesses, and some individuals give guests and visitors "address cards" in both English and Korean. These cards are designed to be shown to taxi drivers.

If you are going someplace with an address that is not commonly known, such as an individual home or small business, it is important to have specific instructions for a taxi driver or precise information about how you can get there using public transportation.

Free-for-all in the Streets

First-time visitors to Korea must be equipped with another piece of information in order to navigate the larger cities successfully and safely: during the morning and evening rush-hour periods the storied etiquette and calm of Koreans generally goes by the wayside. Hordes of people competing for taxies and trying to get on buses typically result in free-for-alls with the fastest, strongest, and most determined winning out. The only way to avoid this situation is to avoid traveling by bus and trying to catch taxies during these extremely busy periods. On virtually all other occasions, public behavior in Korea is as good or better than what one finds in other countries.

Also note that it is customary for "Aegukga" (Aye-gook-gah), the Korean national anthem, to be played on the street through

PA systems at various times during the year. When this happens, everyone is expected to stop whatever they are doing and stand at attention.

When in Doubt

Koreans do not expect foreign visitors to know or abide by the finer points of their traditional etiquette—and in fact encountering a foreigner who behaves exactly like a Korean can be a bit disconcerting to them. They expect foreigners to be courteous but to be themselves.

Ask someone for advice if you do not know how to act in semiformal or formal situations, when foreign behavior could be both impolite and disruptive. Koreans take great delight in showing visitors how to do things, so don't be reluctant to ask. Alternately, simply follow the example set by the event's Korean attendees.

Part III

Cultural Aspects of Korea's Business Etiquette

For Koreans, there is powerful motivation to enrich life and make up for more than two thousand years of living without individual freedom. It is fair to say that present-day Koreans engage in business with the kind of passion and diligence that is often associated with religious fever. But the Korean work ethic can be even more powerful than religion—it is based on the personal, individual drive of each Korean, not esoteric religious precepts.

Another distinguishing factor of the Korean world of business is that it is an extension of Korea's Confucian-based culture. Accordingly, Korean business is primarily human oriented and based on personal relationships instead of the factual, rational, and logical objectivity that, in theory at least, is the primary foundation of business in the Western world.

In this respect the Korean way of doing business is similar to business in China and Japan, but its uniquely Korean elements are clearly defined and comprehensive in their character. The attitudes and behavior of Koreans in their business relationships are more culturally defined, more exclusive, and less forgiving than what is common elsewhere.

International forces began to affect the Korean way of doing business by the 1980s, with an extraordinary cadre of Western-trained businesspeople in the executive ranks of the country's largest corporations. That said, corporate culture in Korea is still very much Korean. It was recognized early on that the distinctive Confucian-oriented characteristics of the Korean people—including loyalty, patience, and an impressive work ethic—were valuable assets that made them dedicated and determined as students and workers. Furthermore, they learned that the Western way of management was generally not compatible with the Korean mindset.

This Part describes Korea's unique business environment and the powerful cultural forces that created it. Western experiences in Korea may vary widely depending on the individuals, agencies, or companies involved, but these topics provide valuable insight into the general character of Korean officials and businesspeople.

The Government as Big Brother

Government bureaucrats or *chongbu* (chohng-buu) have acted as "big brother" in the conduct of business in Korea for millennia. After the new post–Korean War government was formed in 1948 this role was formally exercised through what was described as *chido* (chee-doh), or "guidance," from government officials.

In addition to the various laws that encompassed the layers of *chido* directives applying to business, there were also *nae kyu* (nie k'yuu), or "unwritten laws," that government ministries and agencies resorted to in order to influence or outright control business activities. One of the typical ways *nae kyu* was put to use was by simply not taking action on applications or requests from companies. Bureaucrats who did this engaged in what was called *gara mungeida* (gah-rah muun-gay-dah), which literally means "crushing with one's rear-end"—in other words "sitting on" the applications. Even today it is fairly common for government employees to ignore e-mails, faxes, and phone messages from people, especially those with whom they have no relationship.

The government also controlled business by establishing quotas and sponsoring associations for virtually every industry in Korea. Companies were required to become members of these associations and abide by guidelines established by government committees. Among the most prominent and successful of the associations were those that promoted exports. Others that played key roles in Korea's economy exercised considerable control over domestic activities from manufacturing to wholesaling and retailing, and limited imports into the country.

The role of the Korean government in business has greatly diminished the end of the 1970s, but it remains a virtual partner that must be dealt with. Foreign companies must acquaint themselves with the litany of laws and regulations that cover the spectrum of business in the country.

Bureaucratic Authoritarianism

Despite the democratic facade created by the Korean government and major Korean corporations there is still a strong sense of *kawallyojui* (kwahl-yoh-juu-wee) or "bureaucratic authoritarianism" in Korea's national business management practices. Part of this is an inherent holdover from the nation's historical Confucian ethic, but it also results from the effectiveness of this kind of management when it involves people who have been conditioned to accept it.

Where foreigners in Korea are concerned, however, this

approach to management can be disconcerting because it results in decisions that are arbitrarily designed to favor Korea and Korean companies. Government edicts and policies, weighted in favor of national interests, are still designed to keep a tight rein on business. In turn, company officers exercise what amounts to dictatorial powers in their management, allowing them to make fast decisions and quickly take advantage of opportunities.

Dealing with government ministries and agencies and the Korean way of management can be time-consuming and confusing to Westerners, but enlisting the aid of experienced Korean advisors or consultants can almost always ease this disconnect.

Business Takes a Military Approach

The best way to describe Korean business protocol is to equate it with the protocol of a strictly run military operation, such as the United States Marine Corps. In larger Korean companies the atmosphere can be very much like that of this kind of organization, with rigid formality between the ranks of employees and managers and very little (if any) of the joking and casual chatting that one encounters in typical American workplaces. Like the military, the typical Korean company is a vertical hierarchy with an exact chain of command from the top general down to the foot soldiers. Going over a senior's head, known as *hakusang* (hah-kuu-sahng), is serious business. If the move does not prove to be justified the consequences are serious.

The system of rank in Korean companies is also similar to strict military organizations when it comes to longevity. Employees who joined a company last year, for example, regard themselves as outranking those who joined this year, even though they may officially be on the same level in the company.

Korean management strategy also mimics military organizations with the strict training programs larger companies use to instill in their employees the right attitude and behavior.

Korean-style Management

The main features of Korean management are extreme paternalism and strong emotional ties. Decisions are a combination of top-down orders and plans and strategies worked out by middle management and passed upward for approval. But top management has no qualms about ignoring or disapproving of proposals that come up from below.

Another aspect of management in Korean companies is the role played by blood ties in the hiring and promotion process. Still another is the custom of hiring recruits from the same schools and regions of the country—both strategies designed to enhance loyalty and bring out feelings of elitism in employees.

Company songs, slogans, and a variety of programs, including drinking sessions, are also designed to instill company loyalty and ambition in employees. All employees are expected to demonstrate a degree of *songsil* (sohng-sheel) or "honesty plus sincerity" that equates with the requirements of a military organization. Managers in particular are expected to dedicate their energy and lives to the corporation.

All larger companies have strict training programs that are designed to foster the required attitude in their employees. This training is intellectual, emotional, physical, and spiritual, and when it is complete Korean workers are economic warriors of the first order. These programs include one called *kukki hullyon* (kuuk-kee hulhl-yohn), or self-control training. Part of this training is intended to program new employees to put the welfare of the company above their own. Virtually all middle- and upper-level managers in Korean companies are products of this survival-of-the-fittest approach to training and indoctrination, which leaves them capable and tough-minded.

While obvious efficiencies result from the Korean style of management, it also has a downside. Underlings are disinclined to report mistakes or problems because they know it would upset the *kibun* (feelings or mood) of their seniors. This form of management is also naturally intimidating to newcomers and juniors who typically resort to the age-old practice of *joja sei* (joh-jah say-e), or "lying low," to stay out of trouble.

Dealing with Factions

One element of managing companies in Korea and doing business with Korean firms is dealing with the internal *ppah* (pahh), or factions, that are characteristic of Korean organizations. Factions are of course common in the West, but they can be far more important in Korea than most other countries.

Factions in Korean organizations can originate with family, clan, and regional connections—all of which play more important roles in Korean life than they do in the West.

As elsewhere, school connections can also be the basis for factions in Korean business. There is a lifelong bond between the alumni of Korean and foreign universities, and this bond is especially fundamental in hiring and promoting in Korean companies. This is referred to as *tongchang hoe* (tuung-chahng hoh-eh), or "alumni groupism." Westerners should also respect that in Korea relationships between employces from the same school are significantly affected by graduation order. Trouble may follow if promotions and authority do not follow this order.

Foreign companies with operations in Korea are well advised

to be aware of the faction factor and deal with it before it becomes a problem in their employment and employee management policies. In subsequent hiring, the first Korean employees will naturally favor their own families, clans, schools, and so on, so it is important to maintain a balance from the start. If the employee mix is not culturally acceptable to the Korean employees problems generally occur.

Koreans as Master Communicators

Over the centuries the hierarchical, rank-oriented nature of Korean society made it necessary for Koreans to develop extraordinary skill in verbal communication, including debating and bargaining. This ancient dexterity has remained very much alive in present-day Korea, making Koreans especially good at negotiating business deals.

Koreans bring their strong communication skills to the negotiating table, where there is almost always a major element of stagecraft in Korean bargaining techniques. This floors people who are not accustomed to using theatrics to achieve their goals.

Western business and political negotiators who have been conditioned to depend on facts and logic rather than verbal ability and emotion may find themselves handicapped during business negotiations in Korea. The only recourse in this case is to be aware of and anticipate such techniques and continue laying out your case in a reasonable and logical manner, remaining calm while making positive remarks about the enthusiasm and strong feelings of your Korean counterparts.

Saving Face in Business

The way Koreans go about saving face in business situations often does not conform to Western concepts of what is necessary, right, or acceptable. Korean face-saving actions may include not telling the truth about something, delaying negative reports that will be upsetting to superiors, and arbitrarily taking steps to resolve situations.

Face-saving decisions and actions among Korean employees of foreign companies can lead to serious problems. The need to save face also often causes friction between foreigners and Koreans working in the same company or organization and can result in an impasse, if not a complete breakdown in the relationship.

To avoid a loss of face, foreign businesspeople may not be informed about solutions their Korean counterparts have created to solve potential problems. Foreigners doing business in Korea should use diplomatic means to find out what the proposed Korean solutions are, and try to work out compromises if they do not agree with them.

The Importance of Paying Proper Respect

One of the prime directives in all business, personal, and political relationships in Korea is *chongyong* (chohn-gyohng), or paying proper respect to individuals and to Korea as a nation.

As are most other cultural imperatives in Korea, this respect was a key element in Confucian teachings. Although the power of some other Confucian imperatives has partially dissipated today, an innate need for respect has not and continues to be one of the driving forces in the behavior of present-day Koreans.

Chongyong is an emotional drive and not necessarily rational or logical. Koreans are far more sensitive than most people to slights to their own face or that of their country, and care must be taken to avoid any such slights. Foreigners dealing with Koreans should always keep the concept of respect in mind and refrain from making comments or acting in ways that are or might be offensive. This includes direct criticism, taking a confrontational approach, and acting in a disdainful manner.

This does not mean that businesspeople dealing with Koreans must forego their own standards and expectations of rational, logical, and productive behavior. But it docs mean that they must move carefully and slowly, explaining repeatedly that they understand and respect the feelings of the Koreans they deal with and that their goal is always to benefit these individuals and Korea itself.

Beware of Criticizing People in Public

Koreans do not take kindly to *pipyong* (peep-yohng), or criticism, unless it comcs from someone of higher rank and authority who they recognize as a superior. This is especially true when criticism is publicly given, as this can cause a serious loss of face.

Dislike of criticism continues to be an important part of the Korean character. When Koreans feel they have been criticized unfairly they often feel compelled to take some kind of revenge. Foreign businesspeople dealing with Koreans on any level for any purpose should keep this in mind and tailor their behavior accordingly. Individual criticism should be done in private. Group criticism should be expressed in general terms.

Emotional Ploys to Gain Sympathy

The importance of emotion as a tool in Korean life is not a strictly personal phenomenon. In fact, it is often used by both businesspeople and government officials when doing business with foreigners.

Because the individual rights of Koreans have historically been extremely limited both legally and socially, they have had to depend on skill in both suppressing their emotions and in using them to protect themselves and influence others. One skill that they became very adept at was gaining sympathy, or *omsal* (ohm-sahl), in situations where they had no rights or any other leverage of any kind. This was often the only recourse Koreans had in dealing with family members, government officials, and others.

When used during negotiations this tactic is generally quite obvious, making it possible for the foreign side to devise ways of dealing with it. This can often be done by asking for something they want in exchange for agreeing to the terms requested by their Korean counterparts.

Situational Truth

Formally speaking, the Western principle of truth is based on the facts as they are known without the involvement of any emotional or subjective elements. This concept of truth evolved over the ages thanks to checks and balances that provided people with enough security to allow them to tell the truth without jeopardizing their lives.

There was no such guarantee of security in Korea's traditional culture. As in all authoritarian societies in which the people had no inherent rights, truth in Korea became circumstantial and was based on the situation at hand.

When the first Westerners landed on Korea's shore as a result of a shipwreck on Cheju Island in the seventeenth century, they were astounded to learn that virtually nothing they were told by Korean officials and others on the island and mainland was true. Despite all of the across-the-board changes that have occurred in Korea since the end of the Korean War, this cultural heritage is still discernible in a variety of situations. (It is, of course, especially conspicuous in North Korea, where a totalitarian regime still controls the population.) Today the Korean way of dealing with *chongmal* (chohng-mahl), or truth, continues to confuse and upset Westerners who are not familiar with Korean culture.

Although there are now both customs and laws to protect South Koreans from official sanctions when it comes to expressing the truth, unofficially and informally there are often occasions in work and social relationships when telling the whole truth and nothing but the truth can have serious repercussions. In many settings people are under tremendous pressure to tailor the truth to save face for themselves and others and to keep everything harmonious—at least superficially.

However, the need for and use of circumstantial truth is diminishing rapidly in Korean society, particularly in the international community where situational truth invariably ends up being counterproductive, and among younger generations that are not as steeped in Confucian ideology as their elders.

Still, foreigners doing business or engaging in political affairs in Korea must keep their truth antenna up at all times, particularly in management relationships with employees, to ensure that they are getting the unvarnished facts.

Groupism as Morality

Westerners, especially Americans, assume the people they meet will respond to them as individuals who are able to say and do things on their own. When these people are managers or executives, Westerners assume they have the authority to make major decisions about important things.

However, because Korea's society is group-oriented this is not always the case. The approach to life and business in Western societies allows for personal decision-making and responsibility, and might be referred to as the morality of individualism. In dramatic contrast, the fundamental morality in Korea has traditionally been—and still is—based on *chung* (chuung), or groupism, behaving as a family or group within a company or other organization.

To quote from my book *Korea's Business and Cultural Code Words*, "Between 1400 and 1900 the concept of group consciousness became so deeply embedded in the psyche of the people that its influence is still readily visible today, even though Koreans are no longer compelled to think and act alike for political or moral reasons. In many areas of life opinions and behavior vary greatly, but in such things as courtesy, dignity, respect, pride and ambition, *chung* continues to prevail."

The *chung* factor is still the foundation of management in most Korean companies and organizations. Westerners, accustomed to dealing with individuals, not groups, see this groupism as irrational and tend to regard it as stifling and counterproductive. But given the astounding economic success of Korea since the mid 1950s, *chung* obviously has good points, not the least of which is that it fosters an intensely coordinated team effort as opposed to a mass of individual efforts.

Korean managers and executives are well informed about Western morality and management practices and many of them are comfortable in both Western and Korean environments. Westerners need to achieve a comparable level of understanding of Korean culture—and, in fact, adopt Korean practices that have proven more effective than some of their own individualistic ways of doing things.

Collective Responsibility in Korean Business

In Korean companies the higher up a manager is, the more he or she is surrounded by aides whose behavior is very formal and very precise, like subordinates in a military organization. In small and medium-sized enterprises these managers typically give the impression to outsiders that they exercise power and are personally responsible for the actions of their sections or departments, but power and responsibility generally remain essentially collective.

In Korea's large international conglomerates, however, management is based to varying degrees on Western concepts of individual power and responsibility. The most Westernized of these conglomerates are often led by executives who were educated abroad or spent years in overseas branches of their companies. This said, there is little chance that the traditional Korean way of collective responsibility will weaken much further. It obviously provides both management and the workforce with a kind and degree of motivation that is generally more productive than what exists in the West. Korean businesspeople (and politicians!) are acutely aware of the friction caused by individualism and its negative affects on decision-making and productivity. Westerners in Korea must take this feeling into account in order to develop and sustain harmonious relationships with their Korean employees and business counterparts.

Beware of Depending on Logic

It is important to keep in mind that personal relationships play a significant and often paramount role in doing business in Korea, frequently taking precedence over *nolli* (nohl-lee), or logic. The Western way of basing negotiations, management, and other business activities on facts viewed and applied logically can be upsetting to Koreans, who tend to view this approach as cold and unfeeling.

Of course Koreans can be as logical and rational as people from other cultures, but they generally give personal considerations first priority in all of their endeavors. Broadly speaking, in the Korean mindset people come first and facts—and often profits as well—come second. This is not as irrational or inefficient as some Westerns might automatically assume. In fact, many Western businesspeople were inspired by the Japanese to begin using the same principle in their management in the 1970s and 80s, when it appeared that Japan was going to economically colonize the United States.

When dealing with Koreans on a business level and especially when managing Korean employees, taking their feelings into consideration is vitally important. Rather than focusing on straightforward fact and logic, the ideal approach in Korea, or any foreign country for that matter, is to present your projects and proposals in personal terms, focusing on what it will mean to the people of the country and the country itself. Koreans understand that you have to make a profit, but this approach gives you the opportunity to structure a relationship that they can support wholeheartedly.

The Stubborn Factor

The bureaucratic nature of Korea's traditional political and social systems forced Koreans to develop an incredibly stubborn character in order to survive. Few of the national characteristics for which Koreans are famous have been more valuable to them than this stubbornness, or *ogi* (ah-ghee). This trait continues to serve them well in relations with the rest of the world, particularly in business.

Motivated by the desire to prevent foreign countries and companies from taking advantage of them (and Korea), Korean businesspeople are hard bargainers. But after extraordinary exhibitions of *ogi* they will almost always agree to relationships that are fair.

The Indispensable Go-betweens

It is better, and sometimes necessary, to use intermediaries to discuss and resolve especially sensitive business matters in Korea. The reason for this is, of course, cultural.

In Korea the obligations that family members had to each other and their family as a whole historically precluded them from establishing close relationships outside of their extended families and the few close friends they went to school and grew up with. Outside of this small circle of relatives and friends, there was very little contact between individuals, which meant that Koreans could not simply approach anyone they wanted to do business with because such "cold calls" were basically taboo.

Instead, Koreans had to go through a series of culturally approved steps to develop personal relationships with outsiders, including government officials. These steps could be quite lengthy, involved, and expensive. To make all this easier, Koreans used *chungjaein* (chuung-jay-een), or mediators or go-betweens. *Chungjaein* became an important and institutionalized part of life for strictly personal things, such as the arranging of marriages, as well as for business and political matters.

Professional go-betweens still exist in large numbers today, but their role has dramatically diminished. Nonetheless, they continue to be vital in personal and public matters—from getting into the best schools to finding employment with the best companies or dealing with government entities.

Chungjaein can be helpful to both foreign companies going

into business in Korea and more established companies in their dealings with government agencies and ministries.

The best business go-betweens for foreigners in Korea are individuals who have retired from senior positions in companies or from ranking positions in government offices. These individuals can be found through foreign chambers of commerce in Korea and through private consulting companies that specialize in serving foreign clients.

Letters of Introduction

In professional situations in Korea it is important to be introduced to new contacts and companies by a third-party rather than introducing yourself. For foreigners this rule is less hard and fast—you can introduce yourself if there is no third party available to do so, but you would be well advised to begin the relationship with one or more letters of introduction.

Sogae jang (soh-guy jahng), or letters of introduction, play an important role in Korea because business and professional relationships generally begin with and depend on personal connections. *Sogae jang* can come from well-connected businesspeople, bankers, university professors, business and professional associations, or people with political clout.

In virtually all situations an introduction from a third party helps to open doors and increase the possibility that a successful relationship can be established. Once a relationship has begun, these third parties can also act as go-betweens if difficult situations arise and consensus cannot be easily achieved.

Using Advisors and Consultants

K*omun* (koh-moon), advisors or consultants, can be worth their weight in gold to the foreign company in Korea, as well as to those who require ongoing contact with Korean companies and government agencies.

Because everything in Korea, including business, is personal first, it is almost never what you know that makes a difference. Instead the most vital thing is who you know, how you came to know them, what your relationship with them is, how long it has existed, your sex, your age, and more. The level of personal bias differs with the situation and with the individuals involved, but it is always there.

This is alien to American businesspeople in particular and they are generally not prepared to deal with it in an effective manner. *Komun* can provide insight and advice that is invaluable, as well as use their connections to help you create and build your own network of personal connections.

Business Meeting Etiquette

W hile many Koreans have had years of experience overseas and have become much less formal in their business demeanor, formality is still an important element of Korean behavior in most business meetings.

Appointments should be made at least three or four weeks in advance, as most Korean managers and executives have heavy schedules. Well in advance of your meeting, you should provide your contact with information about your company, your agenda, and the team members who will be attending. Ideally this information should be in both English and Korean.

Care should be taken not to arrive late for appointments with Korean businesspeople. Also, avoid wearing conspicuous jewelry and apparel: Conservative suits, shirts, and ties are the uniform for men. Women should wear business attire.

At formal meetings, the senior Korean team member usually enters the meeting room first. Foreign groups should follow this custom. During the course of the meeting follow the lead of the senior Korean member in how casually you behave, such as removing your jacket if the room is uncomfortably warm.

The Business Card Ritual

Business cards play an important role in establishing relationships in Korea. When doing business there your business card should be bilingual and should be kept in a card case rather than in your wallet or loose in a pocket.

Although there is a growing degree of informality in Korean business meetings, the initial exchanging of business cards is still fairly ritualized. The way in which you exchange name cards is a reflection of your cultural sensitivity and sincerity, and it should be done with some formality.

The very formal way of presenting your business card is with both hands. When feasible the senior member of each group should take the lead in the exchange, starting with the senior Korean member. In a group situation, first exchange cards with this senior person. (It is generally possible to identify him or her by age, position within the Korean group, and by observing the behavior of the members of the group.)

The Korean language side of your name card should always face up when you hand it to someone. Look carefully at the cards you receive and try to associate the name of the individual with his or her title and section or division. In any group there are likely to be two or more individuals with the same family name, so you may need to provide this additional information when referring to someone.

If you are going to be seated at a table for a meeting, do not put the cards you receive away. After sitting down, line them up in front of you on the table so you can refer to them during the meeting. Note, however, that it is considered impolite to write on a person's business card in his or her presence.

Negotiating in Korea

To successfully negotiate with Koreans, you must be informed, patient, and dedicated. Koreans are clever, forceful negotiators who do not mind taking advantage of a weaker adversary. (Traditionally there was also a very strong feeling that because foreigners had so much and Koreans had so little, it was only right for Koreans to get more than the foreign side out of any relationship.)

The polite, harmonious behavior demanded by Korean etiquette, especially during the early periods of getting acquainted, often gives the impression that Koreans are easy marks. But that impression is false. Their politeness masks a shrewd, never-give up, never lose business sense. Korean negotiators are typically blunt and aggressive, with a bulldog approach to asking questions.

When negotiating in Korea it is essential that foreign negotiators know their own products and company, know how flexible they can be, and are as knowledgeable as possible about their Korean counterparts. Some foreign businesspeople attempt to negotiate deals or contracts with Korean companies without leaving their hotel, having only the name and very general information about the Korean side. That is not a good idea. The Korean team will be knowledgeable, well prepared, and active in their negotiating, and you should be, too.

In addition, it is important to bring a team that is up to the occasion. The more important the relationship, the more troops foreign executives should bring along. When selecting your negotiating team, make an effort to find out who will be part of the South Korean delegation. The people you choose to represent your company should match the rank of these individuals, since status is very important and a mismatch may prove embarrassing to both sides. Sending a senior representative can be perceived as a sign of serious interest and commitment, but you want to make sure that the Korean delegation will also include a comparable senior member. If it does not you will lose face.

Since communicating across the cultural barrier between Korea and the West is a demanding task itself, finding a meeting of minds and hearts in a business matter can be a formidable undertaking that requires an extraordinary amount of time and effort.

It is especially crucial that communication be as clear as possible. Many foreign managers without experience in Korea leave it up to their Korean counterparts to deal with the language barrier—including bringing in interpreters if they are needed. This puts the foreign side at serious disadvantage because the loyalties of these interpreters will lie with their Korean employers. Instead, foreign executives should provide their own interpreters and brief them carefully before any meeting, providing in writing the main points they wish to make. Foreign managers also must be careful not rush or overburden the interpreters during negotiations.

When using an interpreter avoid using slang and colloquialisms because they may not be understood. Also avoid raising your voice (a common practice among Americans when they encounter someone who doesn't understand English well). It doesn't work, and ranges from being impolite to insulting.

Negotiations with Korean businesspeople will usually begin with a series of meetings primarily designed to forge the personal relationships necessary to do business together. Do not expect to engage in serious negotiations or make any important decisions during these early meetings. Because of the personal, emotional nature of business relationships in Korea, how one negotiates is just as important as what is being negotiated. Koreans will not—or cannot—come to an agreement until they feel comfortable with the people involved. They must like and trust them. This is true no matter how good the deal is or how much they want it to happen. Foreign executives in Korea have learned over and over again that creating a friendly, positive atmosphere is more effective in bringing negotiations to a successful close than logic, verbal skills, or even an obviously good deal. An uninhibited night out on the town together is almost always worth several days of hard bargaining in a boardroom and is commonly accepted as a routine business practice in Korea.

During these preliminary meetings, higher-level executives will generally be involved. The more detailed discussions that come later, however, are generally left to lower-level managers who are more experienced with the matters at hand.

Information presented during negotiations should be broken up into small segments, with frequent pauses for question and answer periods. There may be extensive questioning and similar questions may be asked on numerous occasions by different negotiators. The foreign team should remain patient; to keep negotiations moving forward it is necessary to respond to all questions directly and concisely. It's also an asset to recap the main points at the end of a meeting.

During negotiations some Koreans will jump from one topic to another rather than follow the agenda. Be patient. If you are confused about their priorities, ask what they are.

In negotiations—and any kind of competition—Koreans are more concerned about losing than most people from other societies. Historically those who failed did not get a second chance. Today any compromise before the very last moment when there is no other option is regarded as evidence of weakness. The standard Korean approach is to do whatever is within their means to win, including revealing as little as possible about the factors involved, switching their position abruptly—sometimes making a 180-degree turnaround—and using the pretext that they must consult with top management. These are often delaying tactics designed to gain a psychological advantage.

Although it is important to have a firm position, insisting on having your own way without any flexibility will be viewed unfavorably. However, being flexible should not imply that you will give in to unreasonable demands. Foreign negotiators should plan in advance what concessions they are willing to make. These concessions should not be made too soon just to avoid a direct confrontation or to fulfil some imagined requirement of Korean etiquette. Koreans expect potential partners to bargain strenuously and giving in too quickly is regarded as a sign of inadequacy.

The personal, emotional level on which Koreans do business may seem to leave the foreign team with no room for maneuvering without seeming to be callous, arrogant, and anti-Korean. Nonetheless, the foreign side should set absolute limits beyond which it will not go, and diplomatically but firmly hold this line.

Another factor that is common to Confucian-oriented businesspeople is an extreme reluctance to say no to a proposition quickly and clearly. Instead they will simply let things drag on, at most giving subtle hints that the project is not going to go anywhere. One of the most common and clear cut gambits for shelving a proposal is to say, *"Keul she"* (kule shuh), "We'll think about it." If the foreign side becomes suspicious that things are not going well and cannot read these hints, their best recourse is to have a mutually trusted third party contact one of the key Korean players unofficially to find out what is really going on. Regardless of the outcome of your negotiations, it pays to avoid burning any bridges in Korea.

When in Korea to negotiate any kind of arrangement it is best to set generous but specific deadlines in negotiating and to be prepared to stand by them. However, foreign managers should never let the Korean side know when their team is scheduled to leave. If this information is known you will likely be informed at the last minute that the Korean team cannot accept your terms. This puts you, the foreign visitor, under tremendous pressure to make last-minute concessions to avoid going home empty-handed. (A similar approach is often taken in labor-management negotiations with union leaders who assume seemingly irreconcilable positions until the last few seconds of a deadline, when they will suddenly accept a compromise.) American executives in this situation will usually either get upset and kill the deal or give in and let the Koreans have what they want.

Any sign of impatience from the foreign team during negotiations will be exploited by the Korean team. Under the best of circumstances, the negotiating process in Korea is usually long and drawn out: A fairly large number of people have to be satisfied with the details of any agreement; communication and understanding take longer across language and culture barriers; and there is an unusually strong element of caution on the Korean side because they feel so strongly that they cannot afford to make mistakes. You will be at a disadvantage if you appear to be in a hurry.

The Korean Understanding of Contracts

Koreans treat contracts and legal documents as memorandums of understanding. Western-style contracts are a relatively recent introduction to business in Korea and have yet to take on the same role they play in Western countries.

The signing of the contract is usually when trouble begins in business relationships between Westerners and Koreans. From the very beginning the contract is interpreted one way by the

Korean side and another way by the foreign one. Foreigners will typically approach contracts as completely binding agreements. As far as most Westerners are concerned, once a contract is signed negotiations are over—the relationship proceeds forward on mutually acceptable, solid ground. But the basic Korean concept of *kyeyak* (kay-yahk), or contracts, is fundamentally different, particularly when government bureaucrats are concerned.

Generally speaking, Koreans sign contracts with foreign executives to officially start a relationship; thereafter everything is still subject to change and negotiation. Koreans do not regard the provisions of contracts to be the fundamental basis of business relationships or even written in stone. Instead, personal relationships and desire for mutual benefit are the foundations of any Korean business arrangement.

To Koreans a contract is essentially nothing more than a symbol of a relationship between two parties, and to keep this relationship current contractual obligations must change in the same way that business conditions and political situations change. For example, as a personal agreement rather than immutable law the terms of a particular contract can become meaningless when the managers of a contractual relationship change. When this happens the contract concerned is subject to the interpretations and expectations of the new Korean managers, who will devise a new set of unwritten terms to govern the relationship with the second party—and may implement these changes without informing the other side.

This is a vital difference in the understanding of contracts that foreign businesspeople must understand. When a Korean executive signs a contract with a foreign company, they are not necessarily obligating their own corporation to uphold the provisions of that contract. The corporation may not accept the obligation if it has any reason not to do so. Instead the contract may be regarded as a personal matter between the managers who negotiated and signed it and the foreign party.

The sanctity of a contract is even less assured where government officials are concerned. When not a direct party to an agreement, they have no qualms about declaring contracts they do not like to be no longer appropriate and in need of renegotiation, or null and void, eliminating the Korean party's responsibility to the contract.

Because government bureaucrats are regularly shifted around—often on an annual basis—contracts between Korean and foreign executives frequently come up for review by people who know nothing at all about them. These bureaucrats have the power to require that contracts be altered or scrapped, and agreements between Korean and foreign companies are frequently affected by this situation. Incoming bureaucrats often feel compelled to demonstrate their efficiency and patriotism by questioning and ordering significant changes in such contractual arrangements.

Not all contractual problems between Korean and Western companies are on the Korean side. Western companies frequently play musical chairs with their top personnel in Korea, breaking the personal relationships that foreign managers have established with their Korean counterparts and making it necessary for their replacements to virtually start over by developing new ties for their companies. When these transitions are not handled thoughtfully and carefully over a period of time (and many of them are not), the switch in personnel gives the Korean side an opening to make unilateral, fundamental changes in the terms of the relationship.

All of this means that it is especially important for any contract with a Korean company to be as clear and comprehensive as possible, and yet flexible as well. A major challenge is to anticipate changes that are likely to affect the operation of the agreement and to ensure that they are covered in the contract.

If the intentions and understandings of the signers of a contract are clear and complete, the two sides are off to the best possible start. One potential problem, however, is making sure that each side does indeed understand the intentions of the other. This may entail a great deal of extra effort in bridging the cultural differences, overcoming communications problems, and really getting down to the facts.

There is also always the possibility that both sides will agree to something they really do not like just to get the contract signed, intending to deal with the issue later. As their approach to contractual obligation is flexible to begin with, this is especially true of the Korean side. It behooves the foreign participant to make a special, patient effort to draw out the true feelings and intentions of their Korean counterparts.

Once a contract is signed it is vital to maintain an ongoing dialogue with the Korean side to stay up to date on their thinking and make the adjustments invariably necessary to keep the relationship on an even course. This is an area in which Western companies often fail because they do not understand the extraordinary commitment required—of both time and money—to adequately nurture the relationship.

It is also true that there is one aspect of the Korean understanding of contracts that makes it a lot easier for foreigners to do business in the country. Once the principals of a Korean company formally commit themselves to a relationship, the degree of honesty, sincerity, diligence, and loyalty they exhibit is extraordinary because their face is affected by their actions. The more face they have to lose the more noteworthy their efforts will be to live up to all expectations.

Professional Hospitality

As in other Asian countries, nights on the town together can be an important part of conducting business and building professional relationships in Korea. In fact, hospitality plays such an important role in the Korean business world that it has been said with tongue in cheek that in Korea pleasure comes before business.

In addition to inviting visiting businesspeople and business contacts out for breakfast, lunch, and dinner, Korean professionals also invite them to hostess-packed nightclubs, karaoke bars, and *kisaeng* (kee-sang) houses. (*Kisaeng* are Korea's equivalent of Japan's geisha—but they predated geisha by a thousand years!)

Foreign teetotalers are likely to have a hard time doing business in Korea, where drinking together at such venues is an integral part of business. There is even a special term for this: *kyojesul* (k'yoh-jeh-suul), which means "business drinking."

Because drinking together allows people to relax and ignore the demands of etiquette, Koreans have been notoriously aggressive in urging newly met businesspeople to drink heavily at after-hours get-togethers. They want to see how their new acquaintances act and what they say when not constrained by etiquette. In this situation the only way to control the amount you drink is by taking only small sips from your glass no matter how often someone attempts to refill it. Another word of caution: It doesn't pay to try to match Korean businesspeople drink for drink—unless you are accustomed to consuming a great deal of alcohol.

The pressure to drink in a business capacity has diminished significantly since the last half of the twentieth century—not only because people are far more aware of Western customs and do not want to come off as boorish and rude, but also because their own social mores now make it possible for them to discard the strict forms of etiquette that historically prevented them from speaking and behaving in a casual manner without being drunk. After-hours entertainment is still an important part of Korea's business environment, however, and individuals who have established mutual trust and respect in these situations will work hard to make each other successful.

Singing Your Way to Success

One of the unique elements in doing business in Korea is the importance of *norae* (no-rie), or singing. Singing solo and in groups has been deeply embedded in Korean culture since ancient times. Long before the appearance of nation states on the peninsula, Korean families would gather around campfires in the evening to sing and tell stories.

This cultural heritage is still important today. It plays a significant role in developing and maintaining personal relationships and also provides an important recreational activity that is physical, intellectual, and spiritual. (The overall benefits of singing are quite extraordinary and have long been recognized in the Western world, but singing gradually disappeared from workplaces in the West when the Industrial Revolution occurred.)

Few foreign businesspeople will spend more than a day or two in Korea without being invited to a *norae bang* (no-rye bahng), or "singing salon," where they will be expected to participate in the singing. Refusing to make an effort to sing is not a good idea; you should willingly participate to the best of your ability—no matter how poor that ability may be.

Koreans will generally take pity of foreigners and allow them to sing in a duo or trio rather than alone. However, the senior guest in the foreign group will usually be asked to sing solo, and Korean hosts are notorious for giving guests no choice in the matter. If you are asked to sing, don't panic if you can't carry a tune. Before traveling to Korea you should, however, make sure that you know the words to at least one very simple song, such as "You Are My Sunshine." I can assure you that no matter how inexperienced you are, how terrible your voice is, or how embarrassed you may be, once you get up on the stage—especially if you are in a duo or trio of friendly, helpful Koreans—the experience is exhilarating and immensely satisfying.

The Annual Greeting Rituals

Korean businesspeople make *insa* (een-sah) or "greeting" visits to their suppliers, customers, and other important contacts during the course of the year. This is a ritualized practice that occurs on a variety of occasions, such as before or after a new product launch, when introducing new contacts, and when acknowledging other new developments in either camp.

These institutionalized and ritualized visits to business and professional contacts (and personal ones as well) are made to reaffirm ties, obligations, respect, appreciation, and the desire to continue the relationship.

Businesspeople in particular use *insa* visits to build relationships and nurture personal ties with key individuals. These courtesy business calls are made on managers, directors, and presidents by people of equal—or near equal—rank.

One of the most important periods for *insa* visits is between 10 December and the end of the year. Another important time for them is the first few days of business at the beginning of the new year, usually between 3 and 5 January. No real business is generally conducted during these *Sebae* (Say-bye) or "New Year Greetings" visits, but they are key for getting the new year started off with a show of friendship and goodwill. There is normally a lot of drinking on post–New Year visits. (The Korean expression for Happy New Year is *Sehae Pokmani Padushipshio/* Say-hie Pok-mah-nee Pah-duu-sheep-shee-oh!)

The *insa* custom should, of course, be followed by foreign companies in Korea.

The Three *P*'s:
Patience, Patience, and Patience

Until the end of the nineteenth century Koreans were culturally, economically, politically, and spiritually programmed to have *chamulsong* (chah-muhl-song), or "patience." This programming was built into the etiquette and ethics of their culture. It was not a matter to be contemplated or debated. It was a way of life.

When South Koreans were freed from Japanese control at the end of World War II and from their own prewar overlords by the establishment of a democratic-style government shortly afterward, they were able for the first time in the history of the country to discard this tradition of patience and become impatient on a scale that must be seen to be fully appreciated. They became obsessed with doing things they had never before been allowed to do, and did them at a pace that was incredible to Westerners.

Their impatience spurred on the growth of the Korean economy, making it possible for this miniscule country to transform into a major superpower in just 30 years. However, this new attitude about patience did not alter the time-consuming consensus approach to decision-making in Korea, or end the need to develop close personal relationships with business partners. And it certainly did not change the cautious way in which Koreans develop relationships with foreigners.

For Westerners, patience remains a prime factor in doing business with Korean companies.

Part IV

Useful Expressions and Selected Vocabulary

Common Expressions

Saying Hello

Hello: *Annyong haseyo!* (Ahn-yohng hah-say-yoh!). This phrase can also be used to mean: "How are you?"; "Good morning"; "Good afternoon"; and "Good evening."
The formal response to these greetings is: *Ne, Annyong haseyo!* (Neh, Ahn-yohng hah-say-yoh!)

Good Morning:
Annyong hashimnikka! (Ahn-nyong hah-sheem-nee-kkah!)

Hello (when answering the telephone):
Yoboseyo! (Yoh-boh-say-yoh!)

Excuse me (to attract attention):
Shille hamnida (Sheel-lay hahm-nee-dah)

Sorry for disturbing you (a formal expression used when entering someone's home or office):
Sillyehamnida (Sheel-lay-hahm-nee-dah)

Getting to Know Each Other

Can you speak English?:
Yongorul hashimnikka?
(Yahng-ah-rule hah-sheem-nee-kkah?)

I understand: *Alket ssumnida* (Ahl-keht sume-nee-dah)

I don't understand:
Moruget ssumnida (Moe-rue-gayt ssume-nee-dah)

What is your name? (said to an older person):
Song-ham-i eo-tteo-k'e toe-seyo?
(Song-hahm-ee eh-oh teh-oh kuh toh-say-yoh?)

What is your name? (said to a younger person):
I-rum-i eotteok'e toeseyo?
(Ee-ruum-ee eh-oht-toh kuh toh-say-yoh?)

Please write that down for me:
Geugeol jeogeo jusige sseoyo
(Guh-guhl juh-guh juu-she-geh say-oh-yoh)

My name is_____ :
I-rum- eun _____ ieyo .
(Ee-ruum eh-uhn _____ ee-eh-yoh)

Here is my name/business card:
Che myong ham ieyo (Chuh m'yohng hahm ee-eh-yoh)

I am pleased to meet you:
Cho'um poepkessumnida
(Choe-ume pep-kay-ssume-nee-dah)

May I have your card?:
Myong-ham han chang chushigesseo yo?
(Myoong-hahm hahn chahng chuu-she-guh-say-oh yoh?)

How do you do?:
Cheoeum poepkke sseoyo?
(Choh-uum pope-kuh say-oh-yoh?)

Where is your factory?:
Tangshin-e kongjang-un odie issumni ka? (Tahn-sheen-eh
kong-jahng-uun ah-dee-eh ee-ssume-nee kah?)

Getting Around

Are you ready?:
Junbi toe ot ssumnikka?
(June-bee toe-eh ah ssume-nee-kkah?)

Let's go: *Kapshida* (Kahp-she-dah)

Where can I get a taxi?:
Eodiseo taekshi tajiyo? (Uh-dee-soh tack-she tah-jee-yoh?)

Please take me to this address:
I chusoro chom ka chuseyo
(Ee-chuu-soh-roh chome kah chuu-say-yoh)

Do you know this address? (to taxi driver):
I jusoka odinji aseyo?
(Ee juu-soh-kah ah-deen-jee ah-say-yoh?)

Please take me to the American embassy:
Miguk Taesagwan-e chom ka chuseyo
(Mee-guuk Tie-sah-gwahn-eh chome kah chuu-say-yoh)

Stop here:
Yogiso torachushipshiyo
(Yoh-ghee-soh toh-rah-chuu-ship-she-oh)

Just a moment, please:
Jamkanmanyo (Jahm-kahn-mahn-yoh)

How much is the fare?:
Yogum-i eolmaye yo? (Yoh-gume-e ohl-mah-yeh yoh?)

On the Town

Let's have a business drink this evening:
Onul pame kyojesul hanjan hapshida (Oh-nule pahm-eh
kyoh-jeh-suul hahn-jahn hahp-she-dah)

Let's go to a nightclub:
Naiteu keulleopeu-ro kapshida
(Nie-toh kuhl-rah-puh-roh kahp-she-dah)

Showing Appreciation and Apologizing

Thank you:
Kamsahamnida (Kahm-sah-hahm-nee-dah) or
Komapsumnida (Koh-mahp-sume-nee-dah)

Thank you very much:
Taedanhi kamsahamnida
(Tie-dahn-hee kahm-sah-hahm-nee-dah)

I enjoyed it very much:
Jeul geowo sseoyo (Juhl geh-oh-wuh ssay-yoh)

You are welcome/Don't mention it:
Chonmaneyo (Chone-mahn-eh-yoh)

Excuse me (an apology):
Chosong hamnida (Choh-sohng hahm-nee-dah)

I'm sorry: *Mianhamnida* (Mee-ahn-hahm-nee-dah)

Saying Goodbye

Give my regards to your family:
Kajok han fe anbu cheonhae chuseyo
(Kah-joak hahn fuh ahn-boo chone-hay chuu-say-yoh)

See you later:
Tto poepket ssumnida (Toe pope-keht sume-nee-dah)

Goodbye:
Annyonghi kyeseyo (Ahn-nyohng-hee kuh-say-yoh) or
Annyonghi kashipshio (Ahn-nyong-hee kah-ship-she-oh)

Selected Vocabulary

Family Relationships
husband: *namp'yeon* (nahm-p'yohn)
wife: *anae* (ah-nay)
father: *aboji* (ah-boh-jee)
mother: *eomoni* (eh-oh-moh-nee)
son: *adeul* (ah-duhl)
daughter: *ttal* (tahl)
grandfather: *haraboji* (hah-rah-boh-jee)
grandmother: *halmoni* (hahl-moh-nee)
older brother (if you are male): *hyeong* (h'yohng)
older brother (if you are female): *oppa* (opp-pah)
younger brother: *namdongsang* (nahm-doong-sang)
older sister (if you are female): *onni* (own-nee)
older sister (if you are male): *nuna* (nuu-nah)
younger sister: *yodongsang* (yoh-doong-sang)

A

accountant: *hogyesa* (hoh-gay-sah)
adaptor (electrical): *adopto* (ah-dahp-tah)
address: *juso* (juu-soh)
administration: *haengjong* (hang-johng)

advertisement: *kwanggo* (kwahng-goh)
affiliated companies: *keiyul hoesa* (kay-yuhl h'weh sah)
agency: *taeriin* (tie-ree-een)
airport: *konghang* (kohn-hahng)
ambulance: *kugupcha* (kuu-guup-chah)
America: *Miguk* (Mee-guuk)
American: *Miguksaram* (Mee-guuk-sah-rahm)
American currency: *Miguk tonghwa* (Me-gook-toeng-hwah) or
    Miguk talro (Me-gook-tahl-roe)
appointment: *yaksok* (yahk-soak)
arrival gate: *tochak kku* (toh-chack kkuu)
ATM: *hyongum inchulgi* (hyoen-gume-een-chuul-ghee)
attorney: *pyonhosa* (p'yohn-hoh-sah)
Australia: *Hoju* (Hohh-juu)

B
baggage: *chim* (cheem)
bank: *unhaeng* (uun-hang)
banker: *unhaengga* (uun-hang-gah)
banquet: *yonhoe* (yone-hoe-eh)
bar: *ppa* (ppah)
barbershop: *ibalso* (ee-bahl-soh)
barter: *mulmul kyohwan* (muhl-muhl k'yoh-whahn)
bathroom: *hwajangshil* (hwah-jahng-sheel)
beauty parlor: *mijang weon* (me-jahng wahn)
beer: *maekjjiu* (make-juu)
beer hall: *pieo hol* (pee-uh hahl)
bellhop: *ppoi* (poy)
bill/check: *kyesanso* (kay-sahn-soh)
birthday: *saeng il* (sang eel)
blog: *bulrogu* (bool-roh-guu)
blogging: *buroging* (boo-roh- geeng)
board of directors: *insahoe* (een-sah-hoh-eh)
book: *chaek* (chake)
bookstore: *seojeom* (soh-jome)

bonus: *ponosu* (poe-nah-suu)
boss: *posu* (poe-suu)
boycott: *poikotu* (poy-kot-tuu)
brand conscious: *sangpyo* (sahng-p'yoe)
breakfast: *achimshiksa* (ah-cheem-sheek-sah)
briefcase: *kabang* (kah-bahng)
British (person): *Yongguksaram* (Yohn-guuk-sah-rahm)
British embassy: *Yonguk taesagwan* (Yohn-guuk tie-sah-gwahn)
broadband: *burodubandu* (boo-roe-due-bahn-due)
browse: *komsaek-hada* (kahm-sake-hah-dah)
browser: *buraujo* (brow-jah)
bus: *posu* (pah-suu)
business: *saeop* (sah-ope)
business association: *hyopoe* (hyah-pway)
business conglomerate: *chaebol* (chay-bohl)
business deal: *korae* (koh-rye)
business hours: *yeongeop shigan* (yone-gope she-gahn)
businessman/businesswoman: *shiropka* (she-rope-kah)

C
cabaret: *kyabare* (k'yah-bah-ray)
café: *kkape* (kah-ppay)
call waiting: *tonghwajung taegi* (tohng-hwa-juung-tie-ghee)
camcorder: *kamkodue* (kahm-koh-duh)
Canada: *Kaenada* (Kay-nah-dah)
Canadian: *Kaenadasaram* (Kay-nah-dah-sah-rahm)
capital (money): *chabon* (chah-bone)
car: *jadongcha* (jah-doong-chah)
cassette: *kasettu* (kah-saeh-tuu)
CD: *shidi* (she-dee) or
    kompaektu disuku (kahm-paehk-tuu-dee-sue-kuu)
CD-rom: *shidi rom* (she-dee-rohm)
cell phone: *hyudapon* (hyuu-duh-pohn)
chairperson: *uijang* (we-jahng)

check/bill: *kyesanseo* (kay-sahn-soh)
China: *Chunggong* (Chuung-goong)
Chinese (person): *Chungguksaram* (Chuung-guuk-sah-rahm)
Chinese language: *Chunggung mal* (Chuung-guung mahl)
coffee: *keopi* (koh-pee)
coffee shop: *keopi shyop* (koh-pee shope)
company founder: *shijo* (she-joe)
company rules: *jimmu kyuchik* (jeem-muu que-cheek)
company slogan: *sahun* (sah-hoon)
competitor: *kyongjaengja* (k'yoong-jahng-jah)
computer: *kampyuto* (kahm-pyuu-tah)
conference: *hoeui* (hoe-eh-we)
connections: *yonjul* (yone-juul)
consignment: *witak hwamul* (weet-tahk hwah-muhl)
copyright: *pankwon* (pahn-kwahn)
countryside: *shigol* (she-gohl)
cover charge: *ipjjang nyo* (eep-jahng n'yoh)
credit card: *shinyong kadu* (she-nyohng kah-duu) or
    kuredit kadu (kuu-ray-deet kah-doh)
currency (Korean): *won* (won)
customer/guest: *sonnim* (soan-neem)
cyberspace: *saibo konggan* (sah-ee-boh-kohng-gahn)

D

date of birth: *saeng-il* (sahng-eel)
debit card: *chikpul kadu* (cheek-puul-kah-duu)
department head/division head: *bu sajang* (buu sah-jahng)
department store: *paekkwa jeom* (pake-kwah jome)
digital: *dijitol* (dee-jee-tahl) or
    dijitol hyongwe (dee-jee-tahl-h'yong-weh)
dining car: *shikttang kan* (sheek-tahng kahn)
dining room: *sikdang* (sheek-dahng)
dinner: *chonyok* (choh-n'yohk) or *shiksa* (sheek-sah)
director of a company: *chungyok* (chuung-yoke)

doctor: *euisa* (uh-we-sah)
download: *daunrodu* (dah-uun-roe-duu) or
  daunroduhada (dah-uun-roe-duu-hah-dah)
downtown: *shinae* (she-nie)
driver: *unjonsu* (uun-jone-suu)

E

ebook: *chonja chaek* (chone-jah-chake)
e-mail: *i-maeil* (Ee-May-eel)
embassy: *taesagwan* (tie-sah-gwahn)
emergency: *wigop* (we-gahp)
employee rotation: *insa idong* (een-sah ee-dong)
engineer: *konghakcha* (kuung-hahk-chah)
English (language): *Yongeo* (yohn-goh)
exchange rate: *hwan yul* (hwahn yuhl)
executive: *hoesakambu* (hoh-sah-kahm-buu)
export quota system: *suchul haltangje*
  (suu-chuule hahl-tahng-jay)

F

farewell party: *songbyol hoe* (sohng-b'yohl hoh-eh)
fax: *paeksu* (pack-sue)
fax machine: *paeksugi* (pack-sue-ghee)
file: *pail* (pah-eel)
first class: *il-ttung* (eel ttuung)
first-class ticket: *il-ttung pyo* (eel-ttuung p'yoh)
flat panel (monitor): *pyongpan* (pyong-pahn) or
  pyokkori telrebijyon (pyoek-kah-ree- tehl-reh-bee-jone)
floppy disk: *pullopi disuku* (puul-roe-pee-deesu-koo)
folder: *poldo* (poel-doe)
foreign patent: *chonmae tuko* (chone-my tuu-kah)
France: *Pullanseo* (Puul-lahn-suh)
French (language): *Pullanseo mal* (Puhl-lahn-suh mahl)
French (person): *Pullanseo saram* (Puhl-lahn-suh sah-ram)

G

geek (computer): *otaku* (oh-tah-kuu)
German (language): *Togiro* (Toh-ghee-roh)
German (person): *Togilsaram* (Toh-gheel-sah-rahm)
gift: *sonmul* (soan-mule)
gift shop: *sonmul kage* (sohn-muhl kah-gay)
ginseng: *insam* (een-sahm)
golf: *kolpeu* (kohl-puh)
Google: *Kugul* (Kuu-guul)
group (of affiliated companies): *jaebul* (jay-buul)
guide (person): *annaewon* (ahn-nie-won)

H

haircut: *ibal* (ee-bahl)
hard drive: *hadu-duraibu* (hah-duu duu-rah-ee-buu)
high-speed dialup: *chokosok-daielop*
    (choh-koh-sohk dah-ehl-ahp)
Hip! Hip! Hooray!: *Mansei!* (Mahn-say!)
home address: *chuso* (chuu-soh)
home page: *hompeiji* (hohm-pay jee)

I

information desk: *annae so* (ahn-nie soh)
instant messaging: *insutontu messiji*
    (een-suu-tahn-tuu meh-she-jee)
Internet: *Intonet* (Een-tah-neht)
Internet connection: *Intonet yongyol* (Een-tah-neht yahn-gyohl)
    or *Intonet chopsok* (Een-tah-neht chap-sohk)
Internet host: *pulobaido* (puu-roh-by-dah)
interpreter: *fongyokkkwan* (fong-yoke-kwahn)
introduction: *insa* (een-sah)
iPod: *Aipat* (Ah-ee-paht)

J

Japan: *Ilbon* (Eel-bone)
Japanese (language): *Ilboneo* (Eel-bone-oh)
Japanese (person): *Ilbonsaram* (Eel-bone-sah-rahm)
Japanese Yen: *Ilbon En* (Eel-bone-ehnn)
just-in-time parts delivery: *kanpan* (kahn-pahn)

K

karaoke: *norebang* (no-ray-bahng) or *karaoke* (kah-rah-oh-keh)
Korea: *Hanguk* (Hahn-guuk)
Korean food: *Hanguk umshik* (Hahn-guuk uum-sheek) or
   Hanshik (Hahn-sheek)

L

laptop computer: *raptop kompyuto* (rahp-top kahm-pyuu-tah)
lawyer: *pyonhosa* (p'yonh-hoh-sah)
limited partnership company: *hapcha hoesa*
   (hahp-chah hweh-sah)
log-in: *roguin* (roe-guu-een)
lunch: *chomshimshiksa* (chome-sheem-sheek-sah)

M

management: *kwalli* (kwahl-lee)
manager: *chibaein* (chee-by-een) or *maenijo* (may-nee-jah)
manufacturer: *chejoopcha* (chuh-joh-ope-chah)
memory: *memori* (meh-moe-ree)
metric system: *mitopop* (meet-tah-pop)
mobile phone: *idong chonhwa* (ee-dong chone-wha)

N

name: *irum* (ee-ruum)
name card/business card: *myong ham* (m'yohng hahm)
name-seal: *tojang* (toh-jahng)
nationality: *kukjok* (kuuk-joak)

network (such as of classmates): *dongchangsaeng*
   (dong-chahn-sang)
newspaper: *shinmun* (sheen-muun)
newspaper (English language): *Yongjja shinmun*
   (Yohn-jjah sheen-muun)
notary public: *kongjung-in* (kong-jung-een)
notebook computer: *notubuk kompyuto*
   (no-tuu-buuk kahm-pyuu-tah) or *notubuk* (no-tuu-buuk)

O

occupation: *chigop* (chee-gahp)
office: *samushil* (sah-muhl-sheel)
office worker: *samuwon* (sah-muu-won)
Olympics: *Olrimpik* (Ohl-reem-peek)
one-way ticket: *pyon-do pyo* (p'yohn-doh p'yoh)
one-way trip: *pyon-do* (p'yohn-doh)
online: *onrain* (own-rah- een)

P

pager: *hochulgi* (hoe-chuul-ghee) or *pipi* (ppee-ppee)
parcel: *sopo* (soh-pah)
passport: *yokkwon* (yoke-kwahn)
personal connections: *in maek* (inn make)
platform (subway/train boarding): *pullethom* (puul-ret-home)
   or *sunggangjang* (suung-gahng-jahng)
podcasting: *patkesuting* (paht-kass-teeng)
police: *kyongchal* (k'yohng-chahl)
population: *ingu* (een-guu)
post office: *uche guk* (uu-chay guuk)
prescription: *chobang* (choh-bahng)
president: *sajang* (sah-jahng)
private secretary: *piso* (pee-soh)
product samples: *kyonbon* (kyoan-bohn)
professor: *kyosu* (k'yoh-suu)

province: *to* (toh)
provincial capital: *to chong sojaeji* (toh chohng soh-jay-jee)

Q

quality: *pumjil* (pume-jeel)

R

RAM: *raem* (rahm)
receipt: *yongsujong* (yohng-suu-johng)
region: *chibang* (chee-bahng)
remote control: *rimokon* (ree-moe-kohn)
reservations: *yeyak* (yeh-yahk)
reserved seat: *chijong sok* (chee-johng soak)
restaurant (American): *Miguk jjip* (Me-guuk jeep)
restaurant (Chinese): *Chungguk jjip* (Chuung-guuk jeep)
restaurant (Korean): *Hanguk jjip* (Hahn-guuk jeep)
restaurant (Japanese): *Il shik jjip* (Eel sheek jeep)
restroom: *hwajangshil* (hwah-jahng-sheel)
round-trip: *wang-bok* (wahng-bohk)
Russian (person): *Soryonsaram* (soh-r'yohn-sah-rahm)

S

secretary: *piso* (pee-soh)
security: *kompyuto sekyuriti* (kahm-pyuu-tah- seh-kyuu-ree-tee)
senior citizen: *no-in* (noh-een)
sightseeing: *kwangwang* (kwahn-gwahng)
signature: *seo myong* (soh myoong)
ski: *suki* (ski) or *skiing* (ski-eeng)
soccer: *chukku* (chuuk-koo)
software: *soputowaeo* (soe-puu-tuu-way-ahh)
spam (junk e-mail): *supaem* (suu-pam) or
    supaem maeil (sue-pam-may-eel)
sports: *supochu* (sue-poe-chuu) or *undong* (uun-dohng)
stadium: *kyonggijang* (kyahng-ghee-jahng)
station: *yok* (yoke)

stereo system: *chonchuk* (chone-chuuk) or
   sutaeraeo shisutaem (sue-tay-ray-oh-she-sue-tame)
stock company: *chusik hoesa* (chuu-sheek hweh-sah)
student: *haksaeng* (hahk-sang)
subcontract firm(s): *hachong* (hah-chohng)
subway: *chihachol* (chee-hah-choel)
subway line: *chihachol noson* (chee-hah-choel-no-sahn)
subway station: *chihachol yok* (chee-hah-choel yahk)
swimming: *suyong* (sue-yahng) or *heom chigi* (hohm-chee-gee)
swimmer: *suyong sonsu* (sue-yahng sahn-suh) or
   suyonghanun saram (sue-yahng-hah-nuun-sah-rahm)

T
taxi: *taekshi* (tack-she)
telephone/telephone call: *chonhwa* (chone-hwah)
   international phone call: *kukjjie chonhwa*
      (kuuk-jay chone-hwah)
   local call: *shinae chonhwa* (she-nie chone-hwah)
   telephone directory: *chonwha ponhobu*
      (chone-hwah pahn-hoh-buu)
   telephone number: *chonhwa ponho* (chone-hwah pahn-hoh)
temple (Buddhist): *chol* (chohl)
tennis: *tenisu* (tay-nee-sue) or *chonggu* (chang-guu)
ticket: *pyo* (p'yoh)
ticket machine: *chapyo chadong panmaegi*
   (chah-p'yoh cha-dung pahn-may-ghee)
ticket office: *maepyo so* (may-p'yoh-saw)
ticket window: *maepyo gu* (may-p'yoh guh)
title: *chemok* (chuh-moke)
tour: *yeohaeng* (yah-hang)
tour guide: *yeohaeng annaeso* (yah-hang ahn-nie-soh)
tourist: *kwanggwanggaek* (kwahng-gwahng-gake)
tourist information center: *kwanggwang annaeso*
   (kwahng-gwahng ahn-nie-saw)

train: *kicha* (kee-chah)
    express: *mugung hwa-ho* (muu-guung hwah-hoh)
    limited express: *tong-il ho* (tohng-eel hoh)
    local train: *pidulgi ho* (pee-duhl-ghee hoh)
    super express: *saemaeul-ho* (sie-mah-euhl-hoh)
typhoon: *taepung* (tie-puung)

U
United States: *Miguk* (Me-guuk)
unwritten government rules: *naekyu* (nie-que)
update: *opdaeituhada* (ahp-day-tuu-hah-dah)
upload: *oprodu* (ahp-roe-duu)

V
vacation: *hyuga* (h'yuu-gah)
vice president: *pusa-jang* (puu-sah-jahng)
video camera: *bidio kamaera* (bee-dee-oh-kah-may-rah)
video cassette: *bidio kasetu* (bee-dee-oh-kah-seh-tuu)
video cassette recorder: *bidio kasettu rekodo*
    (bee-dee-oh-kah-seh-tuu-reh-koh-duh)
video games: *bidio kaeim* (bee-dee-oh-kame)
visa: *pija* (pee-jah)

W
water: *mul* (muhl)
weather: *nalshi* (nahl-she)
website: *wepsaitu* (wep-sie-tuu) or *hom-peiji* (home-pay-jee)
welcome: *eoso oseyo* (uh-soh oh-say-yoh)
welcome reception: *hwanyong hoe* (wahn-yong hoe-eh)
wi-fi: *muson intonaet* (muu-san een-tah-net)
wireless: *muson* (muu-san)/*musonwi* (muu-san-wee)
worm: *wom bairosu* (wahm-bah-ee-roe-sue)

Y
Yahoo: *Yahu* (Yah-huu)

Index

A

Advances, scientific, 16

"Aeguka" (national anthem), 23–24, 76

Age, and etiquette, 51

Airports, Korean, 9

Alcohol, 60–61, 103

Ancestor worship, 15

Apologies, 55

B

Bargaining, 71–72

Birthdays, celebrating, 68–69

Body language, 53–54

Bowing, 51–53

Buddhism, 14, 44–45, 56

Business: alcohol and, 103; advisors and consultants in, 93; annual greeting rituals, 105; business card ritual, 94–95; collective responsibility in, 89; contracts in, 99–102; criticism in, 85; emotion in, 86; English-language e-mail and, 67; factions and, 82–83; friendship in, 33–34, 102–103; go-betweens and, 91–92; groupism and, 87–87; government control of, 78–80; internationalization of, 19; interpreters and, 96; letters of introduction and, 92; logic and, 89–90; management practices, 81–82; meetings, etiquette of, 93–94; meetings, leaving, 63; military organization, as, 80–81; negotiations and, 72, 83, 95–99; patience, 106; professional hospitality, 55–56, 102–103; respect and, 84–85; saving face in, 84; singing and, 104; situational truth in, 86–87; stubbornness and, 90–91

Business cards, 94–95

Business entertainment, 102–103

125